A Phonological Study of the Gwari Lects

**Summer Institute of Linguistics
Language Data
Africa Series**

Publication 24

Marilyn A. Mayers
Volume editor

William R. Merrifield
*Editor-in-chief
Academic Publications Coordinator*

A Phonological Study of the Gwari Lects

Heidi James Rosendall

A Publication of
The Summer Institute of Linguistics
1992

LANGUAGE DATA is a serial publication of the Summer Institute of Linguistics, Inc. The series is intended as an outlet for data-oriented papers authored by members of the Institute. All volumes are issued as microfiche editions, while certain selected volumes are also printed in off-set editions.

Copyright ©1992 by the Summer Institute of Linguistics, Inc.

Library of Congress Catalog No: 92–081460

ISBN: 0-88312-186-7

ISSN: 1040–4406

Printed in the United States of America

All Rights Reserved

No part of this publication may be reproduced, stored in a retrieval system, or transmitted in any form or by any means—electronic, mechanical, photocopy, recording, or otherwise—without the express permission of the Summer Institute of Linguistics, with the exception of brief excerpts in journal articles or reviews.

Cover design and illustration by Hazel Shorey
Cover illustration depicts a Gwari musical instrument

Copies of this and other publications of the Summer Institute of Linguistics may be obtained from

International Academic Bookstore
7500 W. Camp Wisdom Road
Dallas, TX 75236

Contents

Preface ix

Acknowledgments xi

1. Introduction 1
   1.1 Gwari 1
      1.1.1 The people 1
      1.1.2 The language 2
   1.2 Background Information 4
      1.2.1 Purpose and methodology 4
      1.2.2 Linguistic theory 7
   1.3 Findings 7

2. Phonetic Description 9
   2.1 Consonants 9
   2.2 Vowels 42
   2.3 Tones 52

3. Phonological Description 65
   3.1 The phonology of Gwari as a whole 65
      3.1.1 The syllable structure of Gwari 65
      3.1.2 Consonants 66

3.1.3 Vowels 68
3.1.4 Tone 68
3.2 Southern Gbari (GIR) 69
   3.2.1 Phonetic chart of Southern Gbari 69
   3.2.2 Evidence of contrast 70
   3.2.3 Evidence of syllable structure 71
   3.2.4 Rules 71
   3.2.5 Phoneme chart of Southern Gbari 75
3.3 Northern Gbari (GBB) 76
   3.3.1 Phonetic chart of Northern Gbari 76
   3.3.2 Evidence of contrast 76
   3.3.3 Evidence of syllable structure 78
   3.3.4 Rules 78
   3.3.5 Phoneme chart of Northern Gbari 80
3.4 Southern Gbagyi (ARA) 81
   3.4.1 Phonetic chart of Southern Gbagyi 81
   3.4.2 Evidence of contrast 82
   3.4.3 Evidence of syllable structure 83
   3.4.4 Rules 83
   3.4.5 Phoneme chart of Southern Gbagyi 86
3.5 Northern Gbagyi (PAP) 86
   3.5.1 Phonetic chart of Northern Gbagyi 86
   3.5.2 Evidence of contrast 87
   3.5.3 Evidence of syllable structure 88
   3.5.4 Rules 88
   3.5.5 Phoneme chart of Northern Gbagyi 90

4. Glides 91
   4.1 The palatal glide 91
      4.1.1 The phonetic realization of the palatal glide . . 91
      4.1.2 The distribution of the palatal glide 93
      4.1.3 The effect of the palatal glide upon vowels . . . 94

Contents

4.2 The labial velar glide	96
4.2.1 The phonetic realization of the labial velar glide	96
4.2.2 The distribution of the labial velar glide	97
4.2.3 The effect of the labial velar glide upon vowels	98
5. Nasality	101
5.1 The distribution and phonetic manifestations of nasality	101
5.1.1 The nasal consonants	101
5.1.2 The postnasalized consonants	103
5.1.3 The nasal(ized) vowels	103
5.2 Phonological interpretations of nasality	103
5.2.1 Nasality and consonants	103
5.2.2 Nasality and vowels	106
5.3 Nasality and the syllable structure	107
6. Unity of Gwari—Gbagyi and Gbari	109
6.1 Sociological unity	109
6.2 Phonological unity—A recommendation for standardization	110
6.3 On lexical counts and intelligibility	110
6.4 Conclusion	113
References	115

Preface

This volume is a phonological study of the four Gwari lects, Northern and Southern Gbagyi, and Northern and Southern Gbari, with the purpose of coming to a greater understanding of the phonological processes of Gwari as a whole. After a phonetic and phonological description of the lects, the processes of palatalization, labialization, and nasalization are given individual attention as these processes uniquely characterize Gwari. The theoretical framework is traditional segmental phonology.

While the Gwari lects are very similar phonologically, having the same phonemes excepting /ɹ/ and /ɓ/ in every lect, apparent cognate counts and intelligibility testing indicate that, linguistically, Gbagyi and Gbari are separate languages. Hence the use of the word "lects" to describe the Gwari speech forms which include two languages and the dialects within them. The last chapter briefly describes this research and the conclusions drawn from it.

Acknowledgments

To the Gwari people, my most sincere appreciation, honor, and thanks. You, who without exception received me with generous hospitality and gave me your help and time even in the rainy season, have made this work possible. May it bring you good.

I hereby express my gratitude to my supervisor, Dr. H. B. C. Capo, who through his scholarly competence and inspiration guided me to give shape to this study, giving me much-needed help and waiting patiently through many delays to the successful completion of this work.

I am also grateful to my lecturers and professors in and outside the department of Linguistics, University of Ilorin: Dr. (Mrs.) Lawal, Dr. Francis Oyebade, Dr. Awoyale, and Professor Awobuluyi, in the Department of Linguistics; Professor Oludare Olajubu, Dean of Arts; and Dr. Abolade and Dr. Ihebuzor in the Faculty of Education. Their teaching, input, and kindness inside and outside of the classroom has been a real help and encouragement to me.

To the Ajadi's, the Awolola's, and the Orekoya's, my dear friends, my debt to you is indeed great and beyond my ability to pay. May God care for you and reward you in His most generous measure. To Debby Ajadi who worked with me and helped me so very much, what will I do without you?

To the Nigerian people, love. May I leave you only to return soon. Your care and friendship for a stranger teaches me humility. May I so receive those who come to me.

1
Introduction

1.1 Gwari

1.1.1 The people

Known throughout Nigeria for their habit of shoulder-carrying loads, the Gwari people have an agriculturally based economy and live in relatively remote villages. Farming is an important value to the Gwari, who believe that a man is not a man, and a Gwari is not a Gwari unless he is a farmer.

Particularly in the Federal Capital Territory of Nigeria (FCT), the Gwari have been mountain dwellers for generations, some having moved down to the base of the mountains only in this generation. This mountain-dwelling was apparently for protection from raiders, but it is also important to the culture and the traditional religion which worships particular mountains and stones. Luma Rock, near Suleja, for example, belongs to the Gwari and has religious significance to them.

The people are hospitable and peace-loving. Their society is apparently rather democratic and based on the extended family, rather than upon a rigid system of authority. Their focus on agriculture and their nonaggressive attitudes keep the villages small as families move and establish new villages in a search for land and peace. An influx of strangers, for example, is often a trigger for moving, as the strangers will be allowed to come, but the Gwari will move. This choice of the peaceful solution is indicative more of wisdom than of a lack of courage, as they have the reputation of being great fighters when the need arises.

Life for the Gwari is changing, however, as good farming land becomes less available. The creation of the FCT, and the new roads being built there and in Niger State have brought, and will continue to bring, both opportunity and perplexity to the people in these areas.

1.1.2 The language

The Gwari lects belong to the Niger-Kaduna (or Nupoid) subgroup, which, under Greenburg's classification, belonged to Kwa, and therefore Niger-Congo and Niger-Kordofanian. With the classification of the New Benue-Congo, however, it is classified as Nupoid, New Benue-Congo, Volta-Congo, Atlantic-Congo, and Niger-Congo.[1] The closest related language to Gwari is Nupe, while Gade and Igbira are two of the other better known languages in the Nupoid subgroup. Note the three classification charts below.[2]

The Gwari people are found in the FCT and in the four surrounding states of Niger, Kaduna, Plateau, and Kwara. Although opinions vary as to the number, boundaries, and genetic relations of the various lects, it is generally agreed that the two major ones are the ones commonly called Gwari Matayi (or Genge) and Gwari Yamma (or Nkwa). Again, spellings and pronunciations vary on the names of these two lects. In this volume I have referred to them as Gbagyi and Gbari, respectively, reserving Gwari as the cover term for the language and people as a whole.

Culturally, I could discover no difference between the Gbagyi and Gbari other than the fact that the Gbari are more isolated and less interested in the benefits of civilization while the Gbagyi pursue education, are more accessible, and travel more. As the Gbagyi are the larger group and their language is more unified, they have received more attention than the Gbari, few people realizing the existence of two groups.

Greenburg's classification

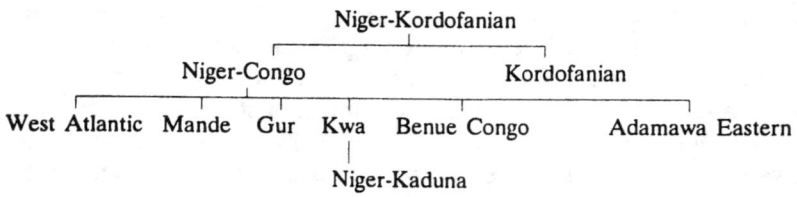

---

[1]The reader is referred to Kay Williamson's articles in The Niger-Congo Languages, edited by John Bendor-Samuel, 1989.

[2]Taken from Williamson pp. 8, 21, and 261 and Blench, p. 307 in The Niger-Congo Languages, ed. John Bendor-Samuel. Not a direct quote.

Introduction

Williamson's classification

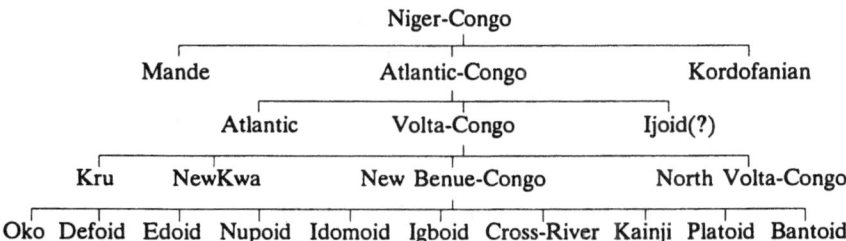

Blench's classification

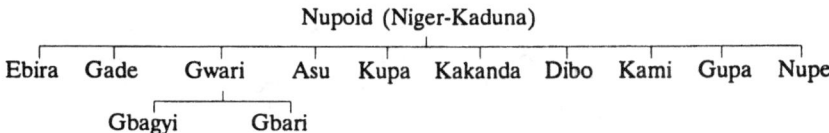

This, in turn, has not encouraged the unity of the two as the Gbari feel neglected and the Gbagyi feel that the Gbari should assimilate to the main group. It is language, apparently, which has acted as a dividing force between them, whether it is formally recognized or not. The 1956 translation of the New Testament, for example, was meant to unify the Gwari and reach them as a whole. The translators were unable, however, due to linguistic differences, to include the Gbari lects in the translation, and it has served instead as a further divisive factor.

Gbagyi. Gbagyi, the larger of the two lects, is said to comprise between two-thirds and four-fifths of the Gwari speakers. It is not surprising, therefore, that it is the more developed and has received the most attention of the two. The Gbagyi speakers can be found from just south of Zaria to the confluence of the Niger and Benue Rivers in a continuous crescent-shaped area. Other language groups are also found throughout the area, with the highest concentration of Gbagyi villages occurring in the FCT and southwest of Kaduna. They are rather thinly scattered along and to the east of the road between Zaria and Suleja, but have maintained their cultural uniqueness. Birnin Gwari LGA (local government area) in Kaduna State was once settled by the Gbagyi, but are apparently no longer a strong presence there. I was unable to visit Birnin Gwari to confirm this personally but hope to do so in the future.

The Gbagyi are very homogenous, with few dialectal differences from north to south.

As the Gbagyi are the most numerous, visible, educated, and articulate of the Gwari, most of the writing about the Gwari has been done in reference to them. Virtually all reference to Gwari can be said to apply specifically to the Gbagyi unless the Gbari lects are directly mentioned by name or locale.

Gbari. Gbari speakers are found to the west of the Gbagyi in a smaller, similarly shaped area. The area reaches nearly to Zungeru, in Niger State, is bounded by the Kaduna River to the North and continues south and east from there through Minna and Paiko to a little past Kwali in the FCT. (See the map on page 5.) There are many more dialectal variations in Gbari than are found in Gbagyi, but intelligibility is high between the Gbari lects. Part of the reason for the fragmentation is most likely isolation, as the Gbari apparently travel little. They were rarely able to give me any information about Gbari speakers outside of their LGA or State, a few not even aware of their existence. This is in contrast with the Gbagyi who could often list all their dialects, their locations, and lexical or phonological differences between them.

1.2 Background Information

1.2.1 Purpose and methodology

Purpose. The focus of this volume is on the phonology of Gwari and on the differences between the lects. It is hoped that the study will shed new light on the relationships between the Gwari lects, and therefore contribute to the information on Nupoid in general. It is also sincerely hoped that this study will aid those seeking to unify the Gwari people. Just as a recognition and understanding of social differences often helps to resolve them, perhaps this study will help resolve the existing linguistic differences.

Methodology. The major tool for data collection was wordlists. Simple sentences used as frames were taken in one village as well, in order to discover the morphological variations across word boundaries, but they were found difficult to elicit uniformly from village to village and were not used for comparison. Short texts of three to five minutes long were recorded in each of the villages where the 420 item wordlist was elicited, and an informal sociolinguistic and mapping questionnaire was taken in all villages visited.

Introduction

A map of Gwari land

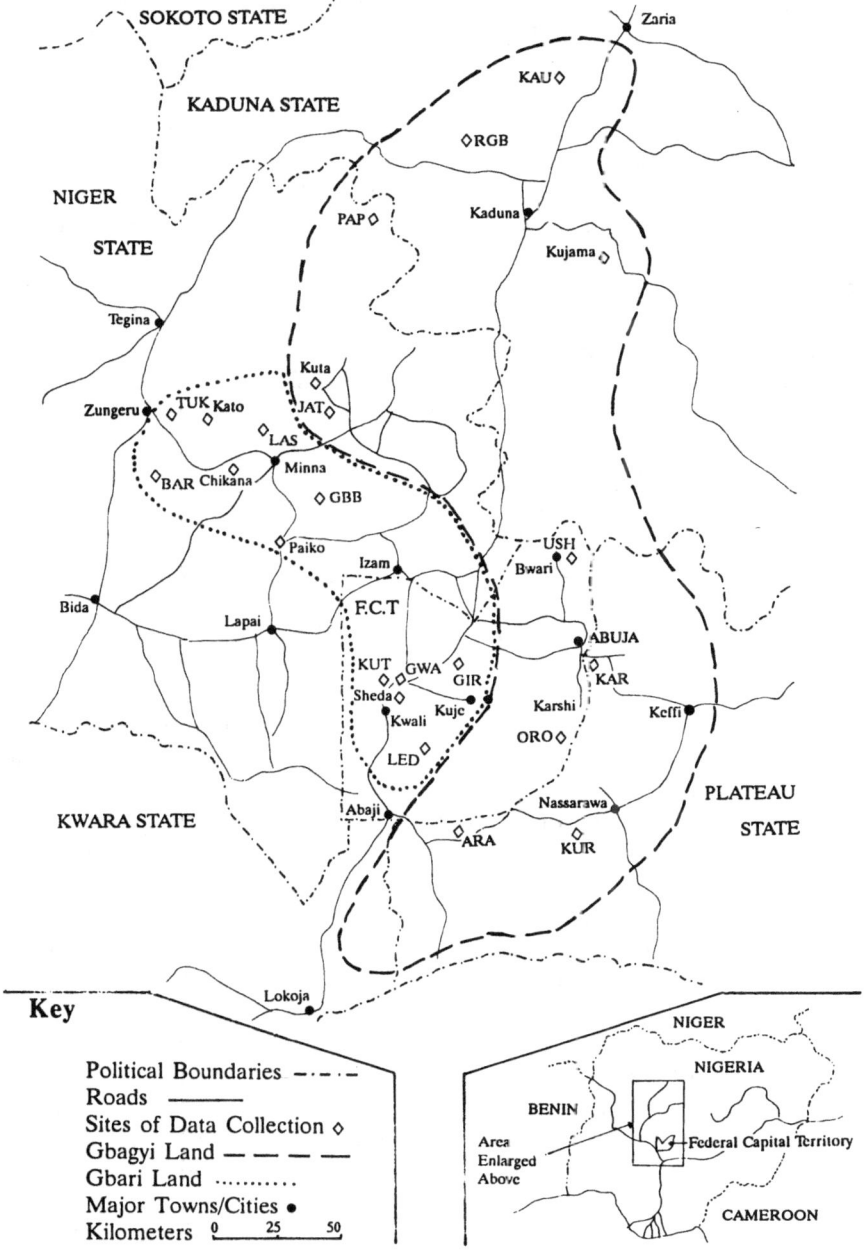

The questionnaire was taken in numerous villages in Gwari land, in order to determine the best places to take wordlists. The Summer Institute of Linguistics Africa Area 170 item wordlist was then taken in thirteen villages throughout the area, and the Ibadan 400 item wordlist (combined with the 170 item wordlist) and a text were finally taken in four villages determined to be good representatives of their areas. In this way the large territory of Gwari land was hopefully thoroughly covered.

The villages used for the wordlists, particularly the 420 wordlists, were selected primarily for language and ethnic "purity," and, as a consequence, were relatively remote. We were almost too successful in our search for language purity, several times having to go to another village because the Hausa or English speakers of that village were not readily available.

Three Hausa-speaking language helpers, Folake Shadare, Halima Danmallam, and Martha Seth worked with me at different times, as I have, as yet, little knowledge of that language, and I was unable to find an educated woman who spoke Gwari and was free to travel with me. Also, because of the linguistic and social differences between the lects, a Gwari helper would have had a limited usefulness.

The wordlists were taken from a person whose first language and whose parents' first language was the lect of the village in question. Both parents had to be born in that village or a nearby one, and the respondent had to be born there. Education was not used as a selective factor. Actually, this person often tended to be the chief of the village, or an elder whom he assigned to help us.

The lists were elicited in Hausa or English, depending upon the level of education we found in the village. Care was taken to find good Hausa equivalents of the words, and descriptive sentences were often used whenever there was a question of understanding. The word was asked and then repeated for confirmation before writing it down in the International Phonetic Alphabet (IPA) script. It was then recorded on a tape in the frame of number, English gloss, and repeated three times.

In this volume, all data are referred to by their glosses and the village they were recorded in. All of the data are from the 420 wordlists. GIR refers to the data elicited in Giri, a village in the Federal Capital Territory between Gwagwalada and Abuja (Garki) and representative of the Southern Gbari (Yamma) lect, and GBB refers to Gbayigan Bussi, a village between Paiko and Minna in Niger State representing the Northern Gbari (Nkwa) lect. The Gbagyi lects are represented in the south by ARA (Araba, a village between Nassarawa and Abaji in the FCT), and PAP (Pappanna, a village southwest of Kaduna) in the north. The southern Gbagyi often refer to themselves as Gbagyi Genge, while the northern Gbagyi may call themselves Gbagyi Kuta, or name a closer village. The name Gbari Ywi, used by the Gbagyi in reference to the Gbari is derogatory and not appreciated by the Gbari, while the Gbagyi do not generally like to be called either Gbari or Gwari. I must apologize to them for using the name Gwari in reference to the group as a whole, but it is the most recognized name and seems to be the best compromise between the lects.

1.2.2 Linguistic theory

Traditional segmental phonological theory is used throughout this book. I had originally intended to use the autosegmental theory for chapters four and five, where glides and nasalization are in focus, but the time available and perhaps my understanding of the theory were inadequate. It seems to me that the features of height, backing, roundness, and nasality are not bound to the individual segment, but are suprasegmental in nature, affecting both the consonants and vowels, and that the autosegmental theory would enable a simple description of their manifestation. This proved to be difficult to describe, however, as the theory could not adequately explain even what was handled easily by the segmental approach. For example, the rule of vowel shortening, where vowels lose their [+ATR] (advanced tongue root) when they are word medial (and there is no glide on the consonants), is a very common phonological rule which I was not able to formulate meaningfully in an autosegmental framework. I still believe that the autosegmental theory could be used to do this and may pursue it further in the future.

1.3 Findings

The findings in this study were very encouraging. While the lexical similarity is very low, and intelligibility testing confirmed that the lects of Gbagyi and Gbari are languages, at least linguistically, the comparison of the phonologies indicate that, with explanation and some compromise, a standard Gwari orthography is possible. Indeed, there was marked agreement in the phonological processes. Although there are other examples of low intelligibility in spite of little phonological difference, it is not the common pattern. Much lexical and grammatical work still remains to be done, however, before recommendations on the possibility and process of standardization can be made beyond the phonological level.

2
Phonetic Description

This chapter discusses the sounds found in the various Gwari lects. The phonetic description and distribution of these sounds are included, as well as a matrix of their distinctive features. While a comparison of the four major lects is found in a later chapter, each sound is referenced to the lect or lects in which it is found.

Although the framework of this volume is not generative, the fully specified features matrices are provided because they are recognized as a valuable aid to phonological analysis, as well as for the benefit of those interested in generative theory.

2.1 Consonants

A phonetic consonant chart of the Gwari lects is given on the following page. The consonants in the chart are attested to in at least one of the four Gwari lects.

Following the chart is a phonetic description of each phone and its distribution. Distribution is shown for each lect in terms of position in the word (initially and medially), and vowel environment. The examples given are referenced according to gloss and lect, with the following abbreviations used for the lects: GIR, Giri of the Southern Gbari Yamma dialect; GBB, Gbayigan Bussi of the Northern Gbari Nkwa dialect; ARA, Araba of the Southern Gbagyi Matayi dialect; and PAP, Pappanna of the Northern Gbagyi Kuta dialect.

Tone is marked as follows: high tone [´], low tone [`], low rising tone [ˆ], and high falling tone [ˇ]. A syllable without any marking is mid tone.

Phonetic consonant chart of the Gwari lects

	Bilabial	Labio-dental	Inter-dental	Alveolar	Alveo-palatal	Palatal	Velar	Glottal	Labial velar
Plain consonants									
Plosive	p			t	tʃ		k		k͡p
	b			d	dʒ		g		g͡b
Implosive	ɓ								
Fricative		f	θ	s	ʃ			h	
	β	v		z	ʒ			ɣ	
Affricate				ts					
Nasal	m			n	ɲ		ŋ		
Approximant				l	ɹ	j			w
Labialized consonants									
Plosive	pʷ						kʷ		
	bʷ						gʷ		gbʷ
Fricative		fʷ		sʷ				hʷ	
	βʷ	vʷ					ɣʷ		
Affricate				tsʷ					
Nasal	mʷ						ŋʷ		
Palatalized consonants									
Plosive	pʲ	fʲ		tʲ			kʲ		
	bʲ			dʲ			gʲ		
Fricative	βʲ						ɣʲ		
Nasal	mʲ								
Approximant									wʲ

[p] voiceless bilabial plosive with egressive pulmonic air. There is usually some amount of aspiration.

Occurs word initially

# __ [i ɛ a ʊ]		GIR
# __ [i ɪ ɛ a ʌ]		GBB
# __ [i ɛ a ʊ]		ARA
# __ [i a ʌ o u]		PAP

[pítà]	'foot'	GIR, GBB
[pì]	'to wring'	GIR, GBB, ARA
[pèná]	'to roast'	GIR, GBB
[pat]	'skin'	GIR
[pa]	'to tie'	all
[pò]	'to roast'	PAP
[pùsé]	'chicken'	GIR

Phonetic Description

Occurs word medially

[e ɛ a u m] __ [e a]		GIR
[e ɛ a o m] __ [i a o u]		GBB
[e ɛ ʌ u] __ [a u]		ARA
[ɛ a] __ [i e a]		PAP
[èpá]	'urine'	all
[kàpú]	'navel'	GBB
[fʷùpá]	'to skin'	GIR
[mèpá]	'remember'	ARA
[àpí]	'compound'	PAP

[pʷ] voiceless labialized bilabial plosive with egressive pulmonic air. There is usually some aspiration.

Occurs word initially

# __ [a]		GIR
# __ [o]		GBB
Does not occur		ARA
# __ [a]		PAP
[pʷáɲũ]	'bag'	GIR
[pʷò]	'mould'	GBB
[pʷákũ]	'bag'	PAP

Occurs word medially

[a] __ [i u]		GIR
[a] __ [i o]		GBB
[a] __ [i]		ARA
[a] __ [i]		PAP
[kàpʷí]	'navel'	GIR, GBB, PAP
[kàpʷí]	'crab'	GIR, GBB, PAP
[mápʷí]	'younger sister'	ARA
[pʷòpʷòɹó]	'toad'	GBB

[pʲ] voiceless palatalized bilabial plosive with egressive pulmonic air. There is usually some aspiration.

Occurs word initially

Does not occur		GIR
# __ [a]		GBB
# __ [i]		ARA
Does not occur		PAP
[pʲaɲì]	'star'	GIR, GBB
[pʲíwà]	'compound'	ARA

Occurs word medially

[e m] __ [e a]		GIR
[e] __ [a]		GBB
[i e] __ [e a]		ARA
[i e] __ [e a]		PAP
[èpʲá]	'moon'	all
[ɲīpʲèjí]	'sun, day'	ARA, PAP
[jèmpʲé]	'feces'	GIR

[k͡p] voiceless labial velar plosive with egressive pulmonic air. There is often some aspiration.

Occurs word initially

# __ [e a ʌ m]		GIR
# __ [e a ʌ m]		GBB
# __ [e a ʌ m]		ARA
# __ [ɛ a ʌ m]		PAP
[k͡pé]	'to put on'	GIR
[k͡pàkʷó]	'door'	GIR, GBB
[k͡pʌ́jè]	'remember'	GIR
[k͡pmì]	'to spin'	GIR, ARA
[k͡páʃí]	'to cough'	PAP
[k͡pè]	'wash body'	ARA
[k͡pmà]	'take off'	GIR, GBB, PAP

Phonetic Description

Occurs word medially

[i ɛ a ʌ o u ŋ] __ [e a ʌ o m]		GIR
[i ɛ e a ʌ u] __ [i e a ʌ m]		GBB
[i ɛ a ʌ o] __ [e a ʌ m]		ARA
[ɛ a ʌ u ŋ] __ [e a ʌ m]		PAP
[mʷákp̂à]	'long'	all
[bʷákp̂mì]	'left side'	all
[tʃiŋkp̂è]	'stool'	GIR
[bʌdʒekp̂í]	'kite'	GBB
[nùkp̂á]	'greet'	GBB

[b] voiced bilabial plosive with egressive pulmonic air

Occurs word initially

# __ [i e]		GIR
# __ [i ɪ ɛ a ʌ u]		GBB
# __ [i e ɛ ʌ u]		ARA
# __ [i e a ʌ u]		PAP
[bíɹí]	'small'	GIR, GBB
[bètá]	'word'	GIR, GBB
[búdà]	'meat'	GIR
[bàɹé]	'cat'	GBB
[béjàkó]	'machete'	ARA
[bè]	'come'	PAP
[bʌwú]	'story'	PAP

Occurs word medially

[e a o u m] __ [i a o]		GIR
[i ɛ ʌ a o u m] __ [i e ɛ a u]		GBB
[i e ɛ a o u] __ [i e a]		ARA
[i e ɛ a o u] __ [i e ɛ a o u]		PAP
[gʷâbà]	'two'	GIR
[tnâbà]	'seven'	GIR
[èbí]	'child'	all
[kàmbá]	'maize'	GIR, GBB
[bɛ́bé]	'breast'	ARA
[ɲàbó]	'request'	PAP

[bʷ] voiced labialized bilabial plosive with egressive pulmonic air

   Occurs word initially

   # __ [i a o u]   GIR
   # __ [i a o]   GBB
   # __ [i a o]   ARA
   # __ [i a o]   PAP

   [bʷùβʷí]   'white'   GIR
   [bʷàdá]   'shoe'   GBB, PAP
   [bʷò]   'be rotten'   ARA
   [bʷí]   'to lose'   GIR, PAP, ARA
   [bʷózùɣʷó]   'thigh'   GBB

   Occurs word medially

   [o] __ [a]   GIR
   Does not occur   GBB
   [e o] __ [a]   ARA
   [ɛ a o u] __ [ʌ a o]   PAP

   [tòbʷa]   'to touch'   GIR, ARA
   [núbʷò]   'belly'   PAP
   [ʌbʷé]   'calabash'   PAP
   [tʃèbʷa]   'push'   ARA
   [òbʷí]   'weep'   GIR

[bʲ] voiced palatalized bilabial plosive with egressive pulmonic air

   Occurs word initially

   # __ [i e]   GIR
   # __ [a]   GBB
   # __ [e]   ARA
   # __ [i e]   PAP

   [bʲi]   'to bury'   GIR, PAP
   [bʲà]   'to blow'   GBB
   [bʲèbʲèí]   'red'   PAP

   Occurs word medially

   Does not occur   GIR
   Does not occur   GBB

Phonetic Description

[i e] _ [i]		ARA
[i a o] _ [i e]		PAP
[bʲí]	'bury'	PAP
[kʷóbʲè]	'kola nut'	PAP
[èbʲí]	'child'	ARA

[β] voiced bilabial fricative with egressive pulmonic air

Occurs word initially

# _ [i e ɛ]		GIR
Does not occur		GBB
# _ [u]		ARA
# _ [i a]		PAP
[βè]	'blow'	GIR
[βùgbá]	'stomach'	ARA
[βàjǽ]	'all'	PAP
[βì]	'follow'	PAP

Occurs word medially

[ɛ a u] _ [e a]		GIR
Does not occur		GBB
[i a] _ [i e u]		ARA
Does not occur		PAP
[έβè]	'knife'	GIR
[núβòmέmè]	'stomach'	GIR
[áβù]	'meat'	ARA
[gnàβí]	'greet'	ARA

[βʷ] voiced labialized bilabial fricative with egressive pulmonic air

Occurs word initially

# _ [i o]		GIR
# _ [o]		GBB
# _ [a]		ARA
Does not occur		PAP
[βʷìjá]	'spit'	GIR
[βʷò]	'be rotten'	GIR, GBB
[βʷà]	'to pound'	ARA

Occurs word medially

[ɛ o u] __ [i e a o]	GIR
[e a o u] __ [i e a o]	GBB
[ɛ a o u] __ [i e a o]	ARA
Does not occur	PAP

[bʷùβʷí]	'white'	GIR
[òβʷá]	'nose'	GIR, ARA
[núβʷò]	'belly'	GIR, ARA
[tnúβʷò]	'belly'	GBB
[èβʷé]	'calabash'	ARA
[áβʷì]	'bush'	ARA
[èβe]	'calabash'	GBB

[βʲ] voiced palatalized bilabial fricative with egressive pulmonic air

Occurs word initially

Does not occur	GIR
Does not occur	GBB
# __ [e]	ARA
Does not occur	PAP

[βʲèfí]	'whistle'	ARA

Occurs word medially

[a] __ [e]	GIR
[ɛ a] __ [e]	GBB
[a] __ [e]	ARA
Does not occur	PAP

[àβʲé]	'fat'	ARA
[ɲáβʲè]	'seed'	GIR, ARA
[èβʲé]	'fat'	GIR, GBB
[ɲāβʲè]	'seed'	GBB

Phonetic Description

[ɡ͡b] voiced labial velar plosive with egressive pulmonic air

Occurs word initially

# __ [a m mʲ]		GIR
# __ [a ʌ m mʲ]		GBB
# __ [m]		ARA
# __ [a ʌ m]		PAP
[ɡ͡bà]	'to pay'	GIR, GBB, PAP
[ɡ͡bmʌ́nù]	'fingernail'	GIR
[ɡ͡bmʌ́ɲì]	'fingernail'	ARA
[ɡ͡bmá]	'swim'	ARA
[ɡ͡bmʲā]	'good'	GBB
[ɡ͡bʌ́ɡ͡bè]	'grass'	PAP
[ɡ͡bmínà]	'feather'	GBB, PAP

Occurs word medially

[i ɛ a ŋ] __ [e a ʌ m mʲ]		GIR
[i e ɛ a o u] __ [e a ʌ m]		GBB
[e a ʌ] __ [i a ʌ m]		ARA
[i e a ʌ u] __ [e a o m mʲ]		PAP
[èɡ͡bé]	'mouth'	GIR, GBB, PAP
[wʲédʒíŋɡ͡bmà]	'dark'	GIR
[zánùɡ͡bájì]	'man'	PAP
[náɡ͡bʌ́jì]	'hunter'	ARA
[dàɡ͡bá]	'elephant'	all
[ʃíɡ͡be]	'medicine'	PAP, GBB
[ʌɡ͡bmʲá]	'fish'	PAP

[ɡ͡bʷ] voiced labialized labial velar plosive with egressive pulmonic air

Occurs word initially

# __ [a]		all
[ɡ͡bʷàɹí]	'house'	GIR
[ɡ͡bʷápà]	'wing'	GIR, PAP
[ɡ͡bʷáɡ͡bmà]	'arm'	GBB

Occurs word medially

[a] __ [a]		all
[g͡bʷálàg͡bʷálà]	'warm'	all

[ɓ] voiced bilabial implosive with ingressive pulmonic air

Occurs word initially

# __ [ɛ a ʌ]		GIR
Does not occur		GBB
# __ [a ʌ m mʲ]		ARA
# __ [e ɛ ʌ]		PAP
[ɓʌɓé]	'breast'	GIR, PAP
[ɓà]	'to count'	GIR
[ɓʌɓé]	'groundnut'	GIR, ARA
[ɓé]	'come'	PAP
[ɓmà]	'break'	ARA
[ɓmʲá]	'surpass'	ARA

Occurs word medially

[o u] __ [i e a o]		GIR
[ɛ] __ [a]		GBB
[i ɛ a o u] __ [e a ʌ m mʲ]		ARA
Does not occur		PAP
[èɓé]	'monkey'	ARA
[òɓmá]	'rain'	ARA
[kútùɓaɹá]	'turtle'	ARA
[ɲìɓagʷó]	'old person'	GIR
[èɓá]	'husband'	GBB
[èɓmʲà]	'fish'	ARA

[t] voiceless alveolar plosive with egressive pulmonic air

Occurs word initially

# __ [a o ʊ u n]	GIR
# __ [a o u n]	GBB
# __ [a o u n]	ARA
# __ [a o ʊ u n]	PAP

Phonetic Description

[tàba]	'tobacco'	all
[tòwò]	'taste'	all
[túgʷò]	'head'	GIR
[tôngù]	'ashes'	GIR
[tnútnu]	'send'	ARA, GBB, PAP

Occurs word medially

any V __ [i e ɛ a u n]	GIR
any V __ [a o u]	GBB
any V __ [a o u]	ARA
any V __ [a o u]	PAP

[mìntí]	'saliva'	GIR
[pútà]	'foot'	GIR
[wìtágʷò]	'hawk'	GIR
[wóʃitoɡ͡bmàɹí]	'twenty-one'	GBB
[kútà]	'stone'	all
[sìntóló]	'leaf'	PAP

[ts] voiceless alveolar affricate with egressive pulmonic air

Occurs word initially

# __ [i ɛ o u]	GIR
# __ [o]	GBB
Does not occur	ARA
Does not occur	PAP

[tsṹŋù]	'bone'	GIR
[tsóŋɣʷo]1]	'night'	GIR, GBB
[tsêntsí]	'tail'	GIR

Occurs word medially

[e a ʊ] __ [a o ʌ u]	GIR
Does not occur	GBB
Does not occur	ARA
Does not occur	PAP

[ètsú]	'rat'	GIR
[mátsã]	'laugh'	GIR
[mùtsʌgé]	'mosquito'	GIR

[tsʷ] voiceless labialized alveolar affricate with egressive pulmonic air

    Occurs once in GIR word initially

    [tsʷíjà]   'push'   GIR

[tʃ] voiceless alveopalatal plosive with egressive pulmonic air

    Occurs word initially

# __ [i e a o]		GIR
# __ [i e a]		GBB
# __ [e]		ARA
# __ [i e a]		PAP
[tʃímʷà]	'tree'	GIR
[tʃógṹ]	'turn'	GIR
[tʃèknú]	'basket'	ARA
[tʃèbʷá]	'push'	ARA
[tʃĩ]	'sew'	GBB
[tʃàbʷa]	'push'	PAP
[tʃàβʷa]	'push'	GBB
[tʃè]	'shoot'	GIR, GBB, PAP

    Occurs word medially

[i e ɛ a u] __ [i a]		GIR
[i ɛ a u n] __ [i e u]		GBB
[e a o u] __ [i e a u]		ARA
[i e a ʌ o u] __ [i e u]		PAP
[gʷâtʃà]	'three'	GIR
[játʃĩ]	'to lie down'	GIR
[fʷátʃùɣʷo]	'village'	GBB
[pétʃè]	'mat'	ARA, PAP
[òɡúʃitʃùáɡ͡bmàjí]	'ninety'	PAP, ARA
[záɣʷʌntʃĩ]	'human'	GBB

[d] voiced alveolar plosive with egressive pulmonic air

    Occurs word initially

# __ [a o u n]	GIR
# __ [a o u n]	GBB

Phonetic Description

# __ [i a o u]		ARA
# __ [i a o u n]		PAP
[da]	'to say'	GIR, ARA
[dàgbá]	'elephant'	all
[díjá]	'pass by'	ARA, PAP
[dókʷò]	'horse'	ARA, PAP
[dùmá]	'duck'	PAP
[dnásò]	'river'	GBB

Occurs word medially

[ɛ a o u n] __ [a o u n]		GIR
[ɪ ɛ a o u] __ [a o u n]		GBB
[i ɛ a o n] __ [e a o u n]		ARA
[i ɛ ʌ a o u] __ [i e a o n]		PAP
[ɛdá]	'father'	all
[ɛdí]	'heart'	PAP
[gʷʌdú]	'go'	GBB
[ádòdó]	'mud'	PAP
[édná]	'river'	ARA
[núgúndò]	'friend'	ARA

[dʲ] voiced palatalized alveolar plosive with egressive pulmonic air

Does not occur word initially

Occurs word medially

[e] __ [e a]		GIR
[ɛ] __ [e a]		GBB
[u] __ [a]		ARA
[ɛ] __ [e]		PAP
[édʲà]	'blood'	GIR
[édʲè]	'wine'	GIR
[èdʲéà]	'blood'	GBB
[kúdʲã̀]	'sheep'	ARA
[èdʲé]	'wine'	GBB, PAP

[ʤ] voiced alveopalatal plosive with egressive pulmonic air

Occurs word initially

# __ [i a]	GIR
# __ [i e]	GBB
# __ [i e a o]	ARA
# __ [i e o]	PAP

[ʤagɓà]	'pepper'	GIR
[ʤã̀]	'to wash'	GIR
[ʤògù]	'to bark'	ARA, PAP
[ʤékpèjákò]	'robe'	ARA, PAP
[ʤì]	'carve'	GBB
[ʤéɹì]	'guest'	GBB
[ʤáʒè]	'return'	GBB

Occurs word medially

[i e a n] __ [i e]	GIR
[e ʌ] __ [e]	GBB
[i e o] __ [e a]	ARA
[i e] __ [i e]	PAP

[zòkowóʤé]	'path'	ARA
[múnʤà]	'sand'	GIR
[kp̂àzéʤè]	'friend'	GBB
[bʌ́ʤèkp̂í]	'kite'	GBB
[èʤè]	'cloth'	PAP, ARA
[ɹíʤìá]	'well'	PAP, GIR

[k] voiceless velar plosive with egressive pulmonic air

Occurs word initially

# __ [ɪ a ʊ n ɲ]	GIR
# __ [a ʊ n ɲ]	GBB
# __ [ɪ a ʊ n ɲ]	ARA
# __ [a ʊ n ɲ]	PAP

[kútà]	'stone'	all
[knúβʷa]	'ear'	GIR, GBB, PAP
[kɲùkp̂á]	'neck'	GIR
[kìnú]	'sheep'	GIR

[kàwé]	'dry'	GIR, ARA, GBB
[kɲí]	'choose'	PAP

Occurs word medially

any v __ [i a o u n ɲ]		GIR
any v __ [e ɛ a ʌ u n ɲ]		GBB
any v __ [i a ʌ o u n ɲ]		ARA
any v __ [a o u n ɲ]		PAP
[ɲíknà̰]	'tooth'	ARA
[mʌkájí]	'dry season'	GIR
[ʤàkí]	'donkey'	GIR
[ɡ͡bákù]	'axe'	GBB
[lákalà]	'stand up'	PAP
[ɲúkùtúkʷò]	'knee'	ARA
[èkɲí]	'ground'	GIR, PAP

[kʷ] voiceless labialized velar plosive with egressive pulmonic air

Occurs word initially

# __ [i a o]		GIR
# __ [o]		GBB
# __ [a o]		ARA
# __ [i o]		PAP
[kʷíjà]	'kneel'	GIR
[kʷoɲí]	'sing'	GIR
[kʷókʷójì]	'old'	GBB
[kʷíja]	'spit'	PAP
[kʷásà]	'to bite'	ARA

Occurs word medially

[ɛ a o u] __ [a o]		GIR
[i a o u] __ [i e o]		GBB
[i a o u] __ [a o]		ARA
[i a o u] __ [o]		PAP
[ɛ́kʷà]	'spear'	GIR, ARA
[lùkʷó]	'duck'	GIR
[ʃikʷíjà]	'kneel'	GBB
[k͡pàkʷó]	'door'	GBB

[jàkʷé]	'mother's brother'	GBB
[zòkʷó]	'path'	PAP
[gnìkʷó]	'market'	PAP, ARA

[g] voiced velar plosive with egressive pulmonic air

Occurs word initially

# __ [i a o u n ɲ]	GIR
# __ [i a u n]	GBB
# __ [i a o u n]	ARA
# __ [i a o u n ɲ]	PAP

[gnĩ]	'pull'	GIR, GBB, ARA
[gɲĩ]	'pull'	PAP
[gna]	'divide'	all
[gũ]	'climb'	all
[gnáɹèpàɹá]	'jaw'	GBB

Occurs word medially

[i e ɛ a o u n] __ [i e a o u n]	GIR
[i ɛ a o] __ [e o u n]	GBB
[e a o u] __ [a u]	ARA
[i e a o u] __ [i e a u]	PAP

[gúzágnà]	'sunshine'	ARA
[ɲàgí]	'food'	GIR, PAP
[ègɲí]	'hawk'	GIR
[ʃĩgé]	'lie down'	GBB, PAP
[ègú]	'fight'	GBB
[ùgútnájì]	'six'	ARA

[gʷ] voiced labialized velar plosive with egressive pulmonic air

Occurs word initially

# __ [a o]	GIR
# __ [a o]	GBB
# __ [a o]	ARA
# __ [i o]	PAP

[gʷó]	'grind'	all
[gʷã̹ɲì]	'four'	GIR, GBB

Phonetic Description

[gʷí]	'open'	PAP
[gʷáʒè]	'right side'	ARA

Occurs word medially

[i a ʌ o u ŋ] __ [i e o u]	GIR
Does not occur	GBB
[i a o u] __ [i a o u]	ARA
[a o u] __ [i a o]	PAP

[lùgʷé]	'big'	GIR
[túgʷò]	'head'	GIR
[nàgʷí]	'hot'	PAP, ARA
[lógʷò]	'cassava'	ARA
[ɹógʷò]	'cassava'	PAP

[gʲ]   voiced palatalized velar plosive with egressive pulmonic air

Occurs word initially

# __ [i e]	GIR
# __ [i e]	GBB
# __ [i e]	ARA
# __ [i e a]	PAP

[gʲí]	'eat'	all
[gʲè]	'see'	all
[gʲáhù]	'to fly'	PAP

Occurs word medially

[a] __ [i]	GIR
Does not occur	GBB
[e a ʌ u] __ [i e]	ARA
[e a] __ [i e]	PAP

[égʲè]	'sleep'	ARA, PAP
[wágʲè]	'to sleep'	PAP
[mʌkʌ̀gʲé]	'dry season'	ARA
[ɲàgʲí]	'food'	GIR

[ɣʷ] voiced labialized velar fricative with egressive pulmonic air

Does not occur initially

Occurs word medially

[i e a u n] __ [i e a ʌ o]		GBB
[nàɣʷí]	'hot'	GBB
[ɲíɣʷánɣʷé]	'senior'	GBB

[ɣʲ] voiced palatalized velar fricative with egressive pulmonic air

Does not occur initially

Occurs word medially

[i ɛ a] __ [i e]		GBB
[ɲàɣʲíɣʲì]	'food'	GBB
[έɣʲè]	'sleep'	GBB

[f] voiceless labiodental fricative with egressive pulmonic air

Occurs word initially

# __ [i ʌ u]		GIR
# __ [i u]		GBB
# __ [i u]		ARA
Does not occur		PAP

[fʌgʌfʌgʌ̀]	'liver'	GIR
[fíjà]	'to sweep'	GIR
[fùɹá]	'hat'	GBB
[fitʃéɹé]	'leaf'	GBB
[fù]	'wash'	ARA

Occurs word medially

[a ʌ o] __ [ʌ u]		GIR
[a o u] __ [i u]		GBB
[a] __ [i u]		ARA
Does not occur		PAP

[táfǔ]	'to fly'	GIR
[ófù]	'lie'	GIR

Phonetic Description

[áfĩnúwà]	'wet'	GBB
[èwṹfũ̀]	'cotton'	GBB
[zàfĩ́]	'corpse'	ARA

[fʷ]   voiceless labialized labiodental fricative with egressive pulmonic air

Occurs word initially

Does not occur		GIR
# __ [a]		GBB
# __ [a]		ARA
# __ [i a]		PAP
[fʷánù]	'cultivate'	GBB
[fʷà]	'carve'	GBB
[fʷíbʲè]	'whistle'	PAP
[fʷàzájí]	'hunter'	PAP
[fʷà]	'cultivate'	ARA

Occurs word medially

[o u] __ [a]		GIR
[o] __ [a]		GBB
[o] __ [a]		ARA
[a ʌ o] __ [i]		PAP
[òfʷá]	'farm'	all
[nùfʷá]	'cultivate'	GIR
[ʌfʷí]	'to die'	PAP
[zàfʷí]	'corpse'	PAP

[fʲ]   voiceless palatalized labiodental fricative with egressive pulmonic air

Occurs word initially

# __ [e]		GIR
# __ [e]		GBB
# __ [i]		ARA
Does not occur		PAP
[fʲẽgʷósà]	'dawn'	GIR
[fʲìtʌló]	'leaf'	ARA
[fʲèɣʷósà]	'dawn'	GBB

Occurs word medially

Does not occur	GIR
Does not occur	GBB
[e] __ [i]	ARA
Does not occur	PAP

[èɓí]	'die'	ARA

[v] voiced labiodental fricative with egressive pulmonic air

Occurs word initially only in ARA

__ [i]

[ví]	'follow'	ARA
[vĩjùkʷó]	'rainy season'	ARA

Occurs word medially only in ARA

[ɛ] __ [i]

[èvì]	'thief'	ARA

[vʷ] voiced labialized labiodental fricative with egressive pulmonic air

Does not occur word initially

Occurs word medially only in PAP

[ɛ] __ [i]

[èvʷì]	'thief'	PAP

[s] voiceless alveolar fricative with egressive pulmonic air

Occurs word initially

# __ [i a u]	GIR
# __ [a u]	GBB
# __ [i ɛ a u]	ARA
# __ [i ɛ a u]	PAP

[si]	'to buy'	GIR, ARA, PAP
[sá]	'to tear'	GIR, ARA, PAP
[sũ]	'to make'	GIR, GBB

Phonetic Description

[sádù]	'pass by'	GBB
[sésí]	'tail'	PAP
[sèsí]	'tail'	ARA

Occurs word medially

[ɪ ɛ a o u n] _ [i e a u]		GIR
[i e ɛ a o u] _ [a o u]		GBB
[i e ɛ a o ʊ u] _ [i e a u]		ARA
[i ɛ a ʌ u] _ [i e a u]		PAP

[pùsé]	'chicken'	ARA
[àsí]	'smell'	ARA
[mĩ́nsà]	'man'	GIR
[bútsū]	'he goat'	GIR
[dnásò]	'river'	GBB
[ɲésùná]	'why?'	GBB
[ʌsè]	'wind'	PAP
[wʲísàkà]	'dawn'	PAP

[sʷ] voiceless labialized alveolar fricative with egressive pulmonic air

Occurs word initially only in GBB

\# _ [a]

[sʷáʃè]	'God'	GBB

Does not occur word medially

[θ] voiceless interdental fricative with egressive pulmonic air. This sound is always in free variation with [s].

Occurs word initially only in GBB

\# _ [i ɛ a]

[θéθì]	'tail'	GBB
[θí]	'drink'	GBB
[θà]	'split (wood)'	GBB
[θì]	'arrive'	GBB
[θì]	'buy'	GBB
[θá]	'tear'	GBB

Occurs word medially only in GBB

[ɛ ʌ ʊ n] __ [i e a o]

[mínθà]	'man'	GBB
[pʌ́θé]	'chicken'	GBB
[èθí]	'iron'	GBB
[g͡bmìnθábíɹí]	'stool'	GBB
[èθe]	'wind'	GBB
[múθànà]	'sand'	GBB
[pʌ̀θóŋbà]	'cock'	GBB
[múθéké]	'mosquito'	GBB

[ʃ] voiceless alveopalatal fricative with egressive pulmonic air

Occurs word initially

# __ [i e ɛ a o]		GIR
# __ [i e ɛ a]		GBB
# __ [i e ɛ a o]		ARA
# __ [i e a o]		PAP

[ʃàk͡pá]	'pot'	GIR
[ʃògʷó]	'rain'	GIR
[ʃíg͡bè]	'medicine'	GBB, PAP
[ʃèɹí]	'witch'	GBB
[ʃi]	'hold'	PAP, ARA
[ʃògú]	'turn around'	ARA

Occurs word medially

[a o] __ [i a]		GIR
[e a o u] __ [i e a]		GBB
[a ʌ o] __ [i e a]		ARA
[e a ʌ u] __ [i e a]		PAP

[ɲàʃá]	'iron'	GIR
[tʃáʃi]	'God'	GIR
[gʲèʃèná]	'mat'	GBB
[kùʃí]	'fetish'	GBB
[ʌ̀ʃé]	'sky'	PAP, ARA
[wóʃã̀]	'heavy'	ARA
[pàʃé]	'urinate'	PAP

Phonetic Description

[z] voiced alveolar fricative with egressive pulmonic air

    Occurs word initially

# __ [i ɛ a o u]		GIR
# __ [e ɛ a ʌ o u]		GBB
# __ [e a ʌ o u]		ARA
# __ [i a o u]		PAP
[zi]	'pour'	GIR
[zɛ̀kní]	'fall'	GIR, GBB
[zé]	'pour'	GBB
[zʌɹí]	'axe'	GBB
[zòkʷó]	'path'	PAP
[zàmʷí]	'forget'	ARA, PAP
[zúkʷò]	'hoe'	ARA

    Occurs word medially

[ɛ a o u n] __ [i e a o u]		GIR
[ɛ a o] __ [i e a o u]		GBB
[ɛ o u] __ [e a o]		ARA
[ɛ a ʌ o u] __ [e a o u]		PAP
[mʌnzè]	'beard'	GIR
[ɲũɣʷózà]	'woman'	GIR, GBB
[k͡pàzéʤè]	'friend'	GBB
[ʌzò]	'beans'	PAP
[bùzùkʷó]	'housefly'	PAP, ARA
[ɛzì]	'oil palm'	GIR, GBB
[ɛ́zà]	'human'	ARA

[ʒ] voiced alveopalatal fricative with egressive pulmonic air

    Occurs word initially

# __ [i]		GIR
# __ [i e a]		GBB
# __ [i a]		ARA
# __ [i e a]		PAP
[ʒì]	'return'	GIR, ARA, PAP
[ʒìʒì]	'black'	GBB, PAP, ARA
[ʒàg͡bá]	'pepper'	GBB

[ʒèʃākṹ]	'pot'	GBB
[ʒènú]	'bush'	PAP

Occurs word medially

[i e n] __ [i]	GIR
[i e a u] __ [i e a]	GBB
[i e a o u] __ [i e u]	ARA
[i e u] __ [i e u]	PAP

[ʃènʒí]	'sky'	GIR
[jéʒì]	'in-law'	GIR
[búʒàɹà]	'groundnut'	GBB
[ʤáʒè]	'return'	GBB
[èʒí]	'egg'	all
[nùβʷóʒȉ]	'think'	ARA
[βʷùʒùkʷó]	'thigh'	ARA, PAP

[h] voiceless glottal fricative with egressive pulmonic air

Occurs word initially

Does not occur	GIR
Does not occur	GBB
Does not occur	ARA
# __ [o u]	PAP

[hùhùjí]	'cold'	PAP
[hù]	'wash body'	PAP
[ho]	'you sg.'	PAP

Occurs word medially

[o] __ [i]	GIR
Does not occur	GBB
[i e a ʌ o] __ [i]	ARA
[i a] __ [i u]	PAP

[kʷókʷòhí]	'old'	GIR
[gʲáhù]	'fly (n.)'	PAP
[zíbìhí]	'village'	PAP
[ɲìpʲéhí]	'day'	ARA
[zʌ́hì]	'oil palm'	ARA

Phonetic Description

[hʷ] voiceless labialized glottal fricative with egressive pulmonic air

    Does not occur word initially

    Occurs word medially only in PAP

    [o] __ [a]

    [òhʷá]   'farm'   PAP

[m] voiced bilabial nasal with egressive pulmonic air

    Occurs word initially

# __ [i ɪ e a ʌ ʊ]		GIR
# __ [i ɪ a u]		GBB
# __ [i ɛ a ʌ u]		ARA
# __ [i e a ʌ u]		PAP
[mʌkʌɹé]	'dry season'	PAP
[máɹì]	'good'	GBB
[mèjá]	'intestine'	GIR
[mìntí]	'saliva'	GIR
[mʌkájí]	'dry season'	GIR
[mínθà]	'man'	GBB
[mùkʌɹé]	'dry season'	GBB
[mì]	'swallow'	GBB, ARA, PAP
[múlà]	'marry'	ARA, PAP
[mèpá]	'remember'	ARA

    Occurs word medially

[k͡p g͡b i e ɛ a o u] __ [p b g͡b i e ɛ a u]		GIR
[k͡p g͡b ɓ i e ɛ a u] __ [p b i a u]		GBB
[g͡b ɓ i ɛ a ʌ u] __ [i a u]		ARA
[g͡b i ɛ a ʌ u] __ [i a]		PAP
[núβòmémè]	'stomach'	GIR
[pìsémg͡bà]	'cock'	GIR
[kàmbá]	'maize'	GIR, GBB
[gùmá]	'bag'	ARA, PAP
[ɓmà]	'break'	GBB, PAP
[k͡pmàmí]	'okra'	GIR
[kàtʃémpá]	'wall'	GBB
[bímà]	'give birth'	ARA, PAP

[bʌ́mú]	'palmwine'	ARA
[dáɡ͡bmàmàɣwé]	'younger sister'	GBB

[mʷ] voiced labialized bilabial nasal with egressive pulmonic air

    Occurs word initially

# __ [a]		GIR
# __ [a]		GBB
# __ [a]		ARA
# __ [a]		PAP
[mʷàɹí]	'horn'	all
[mʷák͡pà]	'long'	all

    Occurs word medially

[i ɛ a u] __ [i a]		GIR
[i a o u] __ [i a]		GBB
[a ʌ o u] __ [i a]		ARA
[e a ʌ u] __ [i a]		PAP
[omʷí]	'mosquito'	ARA
[èmʷí]	'dog'	GIR
[t͡ʃímʷà]	'firewood'	GIR
[dómʷàɹà]	'mud'	GBB
[zàmʷí]	'forget'	GIR, GBB
[òmʷi]	'dog'	ARA, PAP
[túmʷi]	'learn'	PAP
[lèmʷi]	'orange'	PAP

[mʲ] voiced palatalized bilabial nasal with egressive pulmonic air

    Occurs word initially

# __ [u]		GIR
# __ [u]		GBB
# __ [u]		ARA
# __ [u]		PAP
[mʲūŋù̄]	'hungry'	GIR
[mʲūknù̄]	'hunger'	GBB, ARA, PAP

Phonetic Description

Occurs word medially

[g͡b] __ [a]		GIR
[ag͡b] __ [u]		GBB
[aɓ] __ [u]		ARA
[g͡b] __ [a]		PAP
[ʌg͡bmʲá]	'fish'	PAP
[g͡bmʲā]	'good'	GIR
[núwàmʲúknṳ̀]	'thirst'	GBB, ARA

[n]   voiced alveolar nasal with egressive pulmonic air

Occurs word initially

# __ [a u]		GIR
# __ [a u]		GBB
# __ [a u]		ARA
# __ [a o u]		PAP
[nṹwã̀]	'water'	all
[nàgʷó]	'cow'	GIR
[nàkʷó]	'cow'	ARA, PAP
[nàɣʷó]	'cow'	GIR
[nógudó]	'friend'	PAP

Occurs word medially

[t d k g i ɪ ɛ a ʌ ʊ o u] __ [t s z a u]		GIR
[t d k g i ɪ e ɛ a ʌ u] __ [t͡ʃ s a u]		GBB
[t d k g i e ɛ a o u] __ [d a o u]		ARA
[t d k g i ɛ a ʌ u] __ [t i a u]		PAP
[tnâβà]	'seven'	GIR
[gínà]	'burn'	GIR
[gʲèʃéná]	'mat'	GBB
[ágnáná]	'jump'	ARA
[sìntóló]	'leaf'	PAP
[knà]	'fry'	GBB
[g͡bmʌ́nù]	'fingernail'	GIR
[tnútnúnù]	'rubbish'	GBB
[mìnt͡ʃĩ]	'saliva'	GBB

[tunaniʒì]	'think'	PAP
[ʃáknùnaléjà]	'waterpot'	ARA
[gʷúʒēndá]	'witch'	ARA

[ɲ] voiced alveopalatal nasal with egressive pulmonic air

Occurs word initially

# __ [i a u]		GIR
# __ [i e a u]		GBB
# __ [i a u]		ARA
# __ [i a]		PAP
[ɲík͡pʌk͡pè]	'chin'	GIR
[ɲàʃa]	'iron'	GIR
[ɲésùná]	'why?'	GBB
[ɲùɣʷózà]	'female'	GBB
[ɲùkútùkʷó]	'knee'	ARA
[ɲàk͡pá]	'animal'	ARA
[ɲàɲā]	'dance'	PAP
[ɲàbʲé]	'seed'	PAP

Occurs word medially

[e a o] __ [i a u]		GIR
[e a ʌ u] __ [i]		GBB
[i e a ʌ u] __ [i a u]		ARA
[i e a u] __ [i a u]		PAP
[ɹèɲá]	'mat'	GIR
[kʷoɲí]	'sing'	GIR
[kùɲĩkã̀]	'bite'	GBB
[éɲì]	'cloud'	GBB
[g͡bmã̂ɲí]	'one'	ARA
[g͡bmʌ́ɲì]	'fingernail'	ARA
[ɓáɡ̀ìɲáɡ̀bà]	'plantain'	PAP
[úgùɲùmʷáɲùmʷá]	'eight'	PAP

Phonetic Description

[ŋ] voiced velar nasal with egressive pulmonic air

Does not occur word initially

Occurs word medially

[u] __ [u]		GIR
[o] __ [g͡b gʷ k͡p]		GEB
Does not occur		ARA
[ʌ] __ [k͡p]		PAP
[wʲed͡ʒiŋg͡bmà]	'darkness'	GIR
[pʌθóŋg͡bà]	'cock'	GBB
[tsű̃ŋű̃]	'bone'	GIR
[mʲűŋù]	'hungry'	GIR
[núŋù]	'son'	GIR
[k͡pʌŋk͡pʌɹè]	'chin'	PAP

[ŋʷ] voiced labialized velar nasal with egressive pulmonic air

Occurs word initially

# __ [a u]		GIR
Does not occur		GBB
# __ [a]		ARA
Does not occur		PAP
[ŋʷã̀]	'to catch'	GIR, ARA
[ŋʷũ̀fú]	'cotton'	GIR

Occurs word medially

[u] __ [e]		GIR
Does not occur		GBB
[i] __ [a]		ARA
[i] __ [a]		PAP
[tnű̃ŋʷè]	'six'	GIR
[ʃĩŋʷã̀]	'tree'	ARA, PAP

[w] voiced labial velar approximant with egressive pulmonic air

Occurs word initially

# __ [a o u]		GIR
# __ [a o u]		GBB

# __ [o u]		ARA
# __ [e a o u]		PAP
[wá]	'request'	GIR
[wó]	'hear'	all
[wú]	'show'	all
[wêwê]	'new'	PAP

Occurs word medially

[e a ʌ o u] __ [e a o u]		GIR
[n i e ɛ a o u] __ [i e a o u]		GBB
[i a ʌ o u] __ [e a o u]		ARA
[a o u] __ [i a o u]		PAP
[ʌ́wù]	'thread'	GIR
[èwṹ]	'thread'	GBB
[ǹwá]	'I want'	GBB
[kǎwí]	'thorn'	PAP
[tòwò]	'taste'	GBB, ARA, PAP
[pʲíwà]	'compound'	ARA
[nǔwǎ]	'water'	all

[wʲ] voiced palatalized labial velar approximant with egressive pulmonic air

Occurs word initially

# __ [i e a]		GIR
# __ [i e o]		GBB
# __ [i e]		ARA
# __ [i e]		PAP
[wʲi]	'steal'	GIR, GBB, ARA
[wʲôwʲô]	'cold'	GBB
[wʲísàkà]	'dawn'	ARA, PAP
[wʲègbmá]	'darkness'	PAP
[wʲángò]	'sun'	GIR

Occurs word medially

[e a] __ [i e]		GIR
[e ɛ a] __ [i e]		GBB

Phonetic Description

[i e a o] _ [i e]	ARA
[i e a o] _ [i e]	PAP

[knàwʲí]	'arrow'	ARA, PAP
[èwʲé]	'eye'	GIR, GBB, PAP
[έwʲì]	'guinea corn'	GIR
[έwʲì]	'guinea corn'	GEB
[gìwʲé]	'money'	PAP
[gʷòwʲí]	'rat'	ARA

[j] voiced palatal approximant with egressive pulmonic air

Occurs word initially

# _ [i e a]	GIR
# _ [e a]	GBB
# _ [e a]	ARA
# _ [i e a]	PAP

[jikala]	'hard'	GIR
[jéknã̀]	'gather'	GIR, GBB
[jàbà]	'banana'	GBB
[jêjí]	'in-law'	ARA
[jàbó]	'request'	ARA

Occurs word medially

[i e a ʌ u] _ [i e a]	GIR
[i e a o] _ [i e a]	GBB
[i e a ʌ o] _ [i e a u]	ARA
[i e a ʌ o u] _ [i e a]	PAP

[èjí]	'hair'	all
[dujà]	'pass by'	GIR
[k͡pʌ́jè]	'know'	GIR
[tókʷòjí]	'short'	GBB
[vĩjùkʷó]	'rainy season'	ARA

[l] voiced alveolar lateral approximant with egressive lung air

Occurs word initially

# _ [e a o u]	GIR
# _ [a o u]	GBB

_ [i a o u]   ARA
_ [i e a o u]   PAP

[lemúɹì]   'orange'   GIR
[lùgʷé]   'big'   GIR
[lógʷò]   'cassava'   ARA
[lákalà]   'stand up'   PAP
[lídètʃé]   'kite'   ARA, PAP
[lùɣʷé]   'big'   GBB
[lóɣʷò]   'cassava'   GBB

Occurs word medially

[e ɛ a u] _ [i a u]   GIR
[e ɛ a u] _ [a u]   GBB
[ɛ a o u] _ [e a o u]   ARA
[e ɛ a ʌ o u] _ [a o u]   PAP

[gʲélí]   'guest'   GIR
[èlú]   'bird'   GIR, GBB, ARA
[núwàlùgʷé]   'sea'   GBB
[gʷólò]   'kola'   ARA
[kululu]   'round'   ARA
[ɲìtálá]   'tongue'   PAP
[ʌ̀lú]   'bird'   PAP

[ɹ]   voiced alveopalatal approximant with egressive lung air

Occurs word initially

_ [i e o]   GIR
Does not occur   GBB
Does not occur   ARA
_ [i o]   PAP

[ɹídʒá]   'well'   GIR
[ɹógʷò]   'cassava'   GIR, PAP
[ɹèɲá]   'mat'   GIR
[ɹídʒìá]   'well'   PAP

Occurs word medially

[i e ɛ a ʌ ʊ o u] _ [i e a o]   GIR
[i ɛ a ʌ o u] _ [i e a o u]   GBB

Phonetic Description

[a o] __ [a o] ARA
[e ɛ a ʌ o] __ [i e a o] PAP

[kùkúɹí] 'all' GIR
[ʃèɹí] 'witch' GIR
[kukuɹù] 'knee' GBB
[bíɹí] 'small' GIR, GBB
[kútùɓaɹà] 'turtle' ARA
[k͡pʌk͡pʌɹé] 'short' PAP
[g͡béɹè] 'root' PAP
[éɹè] 'sleep' GIR

Fully specified consonants feature matrix

	p	b	ɓ	t	d	k	g	k͡p	g͡b	β	f	v	θ	s	z	ʃ	ʒ	ɣ	h	ts	tʃ	dʒ	m	n	ɲ	ŋ	l	w	ɹ	j
Syllabic	−	−	−	−	−	−	−	−	−	−	−	−	−	−	−	−	−	−	−	−	−	−	−	+	−	−	−	−	−	−
Consonant	+	+	+	+	+	+	+	+	+	+	+	+	+	+	+	+	+	+	+	+	+	+	+	+	+	+	+	−	+	−
Sonorant	−	−	−	−	−	−	−	−	−	−	−	−	−	−	−	−	−	−	−	−	−	−	+	+	+	+	+	+	+	+
Coronal	−	−	−	+	+	−	−	−	−	−	−	−	+	+	+	+	+	−	−	+	+	+	−	+	+	−	+	−	+	+
Anterior	+	+	+	+	+	−	−	+	+	+	+	+	+	+	+	−	−	−	−	+	−	−	+	+	−	−	+	−	−	−
High	−	−	−	−	−	+	+	+	+	−	−	−	−	−	−	+	+	+	−	−	+	+	−	−	+	+	−	+	−	+
Back	−	−	−	−	−	+	+	+	+	−	−	−	−	−	−	−	−	+	−	−	−	−	−	−	−	+	−	+	−	−
Rounded	−	−	−	−	−	−	−	−	−	−	−	−	−	−	−	−	−	−	−	−	−	−	−	−	−	−	−	+	−	−
Continuant	−	−	−	−	−	−	−	−	−	+	+	+	+	+	+	+	+	+	+	−	−	−	−	−	−	−	−	+	+	+
Lateral	−	−	−	−	−	−	−	−	−	−	−	−	−	−	−	−	−	−	−	−	−	−	−	−	−	−	+	−	−	−
Nasal	−	−	−	−	−	−	−	−	−	−	−	−	−	−	−	−	−	−	−	+	−	−	+	+	+	+	−	−	−	−
Strident	−	−	−	−	−	−	−	−	−	−	+	+	−	+	+	+	+	−	−	+	+	+	−	−	−	−	−	−	−	−
Constricted	−	−	+	−	−	−	−	−	−	−	−	−	−	−	−	−	−	−	−	−	−	−	−	−	−	−	−	−	−	−
Voiced	−	+	+	−	+	−	+	−	+	+	−	+	−	−	+	−	+	+	−	−	−	+	+	+	+	+	+	+	+	+

2.2 Vowels

The vowels of the Gwari lects are charted below, followed by a phonetic description and distribution of each vowel. At the end of this section is a fully specified vowel feature matrix.

Phonetic vowel chart of the Gwari lects

		Front	Central	Back
High	[+ATR]	i ĩ		u ũ
	[−ATR]	ɪ ɪ̃		ʊ ʊ̃
Mid	[+ATR]	e ẽ		o õ
	[−ATR]	ɛ ɛ̃		ʌ
Low			a ã	

[i] high [+ATR] front unrounded oral vowel. Does not occur word initially; occurs word medially and finally in all lects.

Word medially

[ɲíkanà]	'buttock'	GIR
[jikala]	'hard'	GIR
[βʷìjá]	'spit'	GIR
[míjà]	'fall'	ARA, PAP
[èʒibihí]	'village'	ARA
[gìwʲé]	'money'	ARA
[kɲík͡pà]	'neck'	GBB
[wʲi]	'steal'	GBB
[ʃikʷíjà]	'kneel'	GBB
[tunaniʒì]	'think'	PAP
[gnìkʷó]	'market'	PAP
[ògúʃìknú]	'fifty'	PAP

Word finally

[èbí]	'child'	GIR, PAP
[si]	'buy'	GIR, GIR
[áɲì]	'soup'	GIR
[pí]	'wring'	ARA
[ʃákwohì]	'God'	ARA
[bʷĩbʷí]	'white'	PAP
[àmʷí]	'dog'	GBB

[bɪnáʲ]	'body'	GBB
[èk͡pmì]	'abuse'	GBB
[àgbámì]	'door'	PAP
[ʒîʒî]	'black'	PAP
[gbmáɲìgbmî]	'fingernail'	PAP

[ɪ]   high [-ATR] front unrounded oral vowel. Does not occur word initially or finally; occurs word medially in all lects.

[pítà]	'foot'	all
[gbmɪná]	'feather'	PAP, GIR
[mínθà]	'man'	GBB
[pítàbʷádà]	'leg'	GBB
[bídà]	'meat'	GBB
[mítàɹà]	'tongue'	GBB
[mìntʃĩ]	'saliva'	ARA, GBB
[gbmínùkũ]	'fingernail'	PAP
[gbmìnθábíɹí]	'stool'	PAP

[e]   mid [+ATR] front unrounded oral vowel. Occurs in all positions in all lects.

Word initially

[édʲà]	'blood'	GIR
[emí]	'defecate'	GIR
[èbʲé]	'fat'	GIR
[égʲè]	'sleep'	ARA
[ewʲí]	'guinea corn'	ARA
[èwʲè]	'lizard'	ARA
[ejà]	'mother'	PAP
[èwó]	'money'	GBB
[èwʲé]	'eye'	all
[èjá]	'thing'	GBB, ARA
[èwʲi]	'crocodile'	PAP
[èdʒé]	'material'	ARA
[èpʲá]	'moon'	GIR, GBB, PAP
[ègbmíjà]	'fish'	ARA

Word medially

[ʃéwò]	'fish'	GIR
[wʲedʒiŋgbmà]	'darkness'	GIR
[k͡pèjá]	'cover'	GIR
[béjàkó]	'machete'	ARA
[sètʃé]	'blow'	ARA
[wʲêtò]	'wet'	ARA
[bʲèíbʲèí]	'red'	PAP
[ɲésùná]	'why'	GBB
[ʃáʃeʒí]	'sky'	GBB
[ŋáɹèpàɹá]	'jaw'	GBB
[ɲìpʲéjì]	'sun'	PAP
[tʃeòkú]	'basket'	PAP
[wʲêwò]	'cold'	PAP
[wêwê]	'new'	PAP

Word finally

[èsé]	'wind'	GIR
[gápè]	'jaw'	GIR
[sètʃé]	'blow'	ARA
[edʒe]	'wine'	ARA
[ʃíɓè]	'medicine'	ARA
[súk͡pʌɹè]	'stool'	PAP
[kàk͡pé]	'basket'	GBB
[dàwʲe]	'want'	GBB
[ʃíg͡bè]	'medicine'	GBB
[èbé]	'knife'	PAP
[èbe]	'monkey'	PAP

[ɛ] mid [-ATR] front unrounded oral vowel. Occurs word initially and medially in all lects; does not occur word finally.

Word initially

[ɛ́tsù]	'king'	GIR
[ɛdnà]	'fear'	GIR, ARA, PAP
[ɛ̀dá]	'father'	GIR, GBB, ARA
[ɛ́bè]	'knife'	ARA
[ɛ̀dná]	'river'	ARA, PAP
[ɛ́bʷà]	'nose'	GBB

[ɛzì]	'oil palm'	GBB
[ɛ́ɓè]	'mouth'	PAP
[ɛnú]	'husband'	PAP

Word medially

[mùtsɛ́gé]	'mosquito'	GIR
[sɛ̀nʒí]	'sky'	GIR
[pɛ̀ná]	'roast'	GIR
[k͡pémà]	'dwell'	ARA
[θéθì]	'tail'	GBB
[ɡ͡bɛɹè]	'root'	GBB, PAP
[k͡pɛ̀ɹéɹé]	'round'	PAP
[sɛ̀sí]	'tail'	ARA

[a] low central unrounded oral vowel. Occurs in all positions in all lects.

Word initially

[áɲìgʷózà]	'female'	GIR
[adá]	'machete'	GIR
[ànú]	'full'	GIR, GBB
[ámĩ̀]	'blood'	ARA, PAP
[àmʷí]	'dog'	GBB
[àɓmí]	'intestine'	GBB, ARA
[àɓámì]	'door'	PAP
[ajàknṹ]	'house'	ARA, PAP

Word medially

[nàgáɓá]	'crocodile'	GIR
[ɲíkanà]	'buttock'	GIR
[dàɓá]	'elephant'	all
[tnâbà]	'seven'	GIR, PAP
[ʒáβʷì]	'bush'	ARA
[kútùɓaɹà]	'turtle'	ARA
[táɹí]	'bow'	GBB
[míjasṹ]	'stink'	GBB
[k͡pàkʷó]	'door'	GBB
[kâwé]	'dry'	GBB
[lákalà]	'leave'	PAP
[kàpʷí]	'navel'	PAP

Word finally

[kɲùk͡pá]	'neck'	GIR
[jikala]	'hard'	GIR
[édʲà]	'blood'	GIR
[òβʷá]	'nose'	ARA
[òbʷá]	'arm'	ARA
[bima]	'give birth'	ARA
[okà]	'snail'	ARA
[kàtʃémpá]	'wall'	GBB
[la]	'carry'	GBB
[pàtà]	'skin'	GBB
[èpʲá]	'moon'	PAP
[la]	'take'	PAP
[éknà]	'thorn'	PAP

[ʌ] mid [-ATR] back unrounded oral vowel. Occurs word initially and medially in all lects; does not occur word finally.

Word initially

[ʌ́wù]	'thread'	GIR
[ʌpá]	'urine'	ARA
[ʌmʷi]	'dog'	ARA, PAP
[ʌ́zò]	'beans'	PAP
[ʌmʷi]	'mosquito'	PAP
[ʌg͡bé]	'mouth'	GBB

Word medially

[bʌ́mú]	'palmwine'	ARA
[ník͡pʌk͡pè]	'chin'	GIR
[sàk͡pʌgʲé]	'salt'	ARA
[bʌ̀wú]	'story'	ARA, PAP
[bʌ́βé]	'breast'	GBB, PAP
[mùkʌɹé]	'dry season'	GBB, PAP
[g͡bʌɹi]	'doctor'	GBB
[k͡pʌ́jè]	'know'	GIR, ARA, PAP

Phonetic Description 47

[o] mid [+ATR] back rounded oral vowel. Occurs in all positions in all lects.

Word initially

[ófʷà]	'farm'	GIR
[osú]	'bee'	GIR, ARA
[òdú]	'heart'	GIR, ARA
[ólà]	'sea'	ARA
[óbʷa]	'nose'	PAP
[ófù]	'lie'	GBB
[òwá]	'snake'	GBB, ARA
[òknū]	'war'	GBB, PAP
[òhʷá]	'farm'	PAP
[ogù]	'fight'	PAP

Word medially

[tówò]	'thirst'	GIR
[kʷoɲī]	'sing'	GIR
[núβòmɛ́mɛ̀]	'stomach'	GIR
[wóʃã̀]	'heavy'	ARA
[ʃákʷohí]	'God'	ARA
[dómʷàɹà]	'mud'	GBB
[ɓègʷósà]	'dawn'	GBB
[pòpòɹó]	'toad'	GBB
[sìntʌ́ló]	'leaf'	PAP
[gʷògʷò]	'hawk'	ARA, PAP

Word finally

[k͡pàkʷó]	'door'	GIR
[zo]	'finish'	GIR
[ʃéwò]	'fish'	GIR
[jákʷonó]	'mother's brother'	ARA
[zòkʷo]	'press'	ARA
[dókʷò]	'horse'	ARA, PAP
[tʃĩgʷó]	'head'	GBB
[ʃègʷó]	'rain'	GBB
[wĵôwĵò]	'cold'	GBB
[mʷàbɛ́ɹèlo]	'many'	PAP
[nàkʷó]	'cow'	PAP
[lŏ]	'enter'	ARA

[ʊ] high [-ATR] back unrounded oral vowel. Occurs word medially in all lects; does not occur word initially or finally.

Word medially

[kʊkúɹí]	'round'	GIR
[kʊkʊɹù]	'knee'	GBB
[g͡bmínʊkṹ]	'fingernail'	GBB
[pʊ̀sé]	'chicken'	ARA
[pʊ́tà]	'foot'	ARA
[mʊ̀tá]	'grinding stone'	PAP

[u] high [+ATR] back rounded oral vowel. Occurs word initially in ARA and PAP; occurs word medially and finally in all lects.

Word initially

[ùgútnájì]	'six'	ARA, PAP
[ùgʷáwòtʃéàtà]	'thirteen'	PAP
[ùgʷâwòtʃâtà]	'thirteen'	ARA

Word medially

[túgʷò]	'head'	GIR
[láɲugó]	'marry'	GIR
[kùtʃi]	'fetish'	GIR
[músìwʲí]	'cat'	ARA, PAP
[kululu]	'round'	ARA
[búɹèkétʃé]	'dust'	GBB
[èsugʲí]	'king'	GBB
[lùbá]	'guinea fowl'	GBB
[bútukṹ]	'dust'	PAP
[gùmá]	'bag'	ARA, PAP

Word finally

[kìnú]	'sheep'	GIR
[kululu]	'round'	GIR
[ɛnáwù]	'extinguish'	GIR
[èlú]	'bird'	ARA
[áβù]	'meat'	ARA
[ʒàbúdú]	'waterpot'	GBB
[náwù]	'smoke'	GBB

Phonetic Description

[tnútnú]	'send'	PAP
[k͡pásù]	'star'	PAP

[ĩ] high [+ATR] front unrounded nasalized vowel. Does not occur word initially; occurs word medially and finally in all lects.

Word medially

[ɲĩgã]	'tooth'	GIR
[wĩŋgbè]	'thief'	GIR
[gnĩgʷó]	'market'	GIR
[vĩjùkʷó]	'rainy season'	ARA
[ʃĩɓé]	'descend'	ARA
[ɲĩknã]	'tooth'	GBB, ARA
[gĩɹĩ]	'mortar'	GBB
[fĩtʃéɹé]	'leaf'	GBB
[àjĩkʷò]	'sing'	PAP
[ɲĩkʷózá]	'woman'	PAP

Word finally

[èmĩ]	'dew'	GIR, GBB
[sĩ]	'drink'	GIR, ARA
[ɓmãɲĩ]	'one'	ARA
[g͡baɹĩ]	'he goat'	PAP
[èɲĩ]	'sing'	GBB
[gnĩ]	'pull'	GBB, ARA
[kãwĩ]	'thorn'	PAP

[ĭ] high [−ATR] front unrounded nasalized vowel. Does not occur word initially or finally; occurs word medially in GIR and ARA.

[mĭnsà]	'man'	GIR
[mĭtà]	'grinding stone'	ARA

[ẽ] mid [+ATR] front unrounded nasalized vowel. Does not occur word initially; occurs word medially in GIR and ARA, and word finally in GIR.

Word medially

[ʃẽwṵ]	'waterpot'	GIR
[ɓẽgʷósà]	'dawn'	GIR
[gʷúʒẽndá]	'witch'	ARA

Word finally

| [knṵŋʷẽ] | 'six' | GIR |
| [mẽ] | 'build, mould' | GIR |

[ɛ̃] mid [-ATR] front unrounded nasalized vowel. Does not occur word initially or finally; occurs word medially in GIR.

| [tɛ̃tí] | 'tail' | GIR |

[ã] low central unrounded nasalized vowel. Does not occur word initially; occurs word medially and finally in all lects.

Word medially

[sãŋʷà]	'grass'	GIR
[ɲìɓãgʷó]	'old person'	GIR
[gʷãbà]	'two'	GIR
[sãk͡pʌgʲé]	'salt'	ARA
[ũgʷãbà]	'two'	ARA
[ɲãk͡pàjì]	'animal'	GBB
[ʒèʃãkṵ]	'pot'	GBB
[ɲãɲá]	'dance'	PAP
[sãk͡pʌɹé]	'salt'	PAP
[ògʷãbà]	'two'	PAP

Word finally

[k͡pèjã]	'to cover'	GIR
[ɠbmʲã]	'good'	GIR, GBB
[mátsã]	'laugh'	GIR
[ɓmʲã]	'good'	ARA
[sàmã]	'to laugh'	GBB, ARA, PAP

Phonetic Description

[ɲĩknã̀]	'tooth'	GBB, ARA
[jĩknã̀]	'tooth'	PAP
[nṹwã̀]	'water'	ARA, PAP

[õ] mid [+ATR] back rounded nasalized vowel. Does not occur word initially or finally; occurs word medially in GIR and GBB.

[tʃõngʷó]	'night'	GIR
[tsóngʷó]	'night'	GBB

[ʊ̃] high [−ATR] back unrounded nasalized vowel. Does not occur word initially or finally; occurs word medially in GBB and ARA.

[wʲèkʊ̃nú]	'lizard'	GBB
[sʊ̀kʊ́]	'bone'	ARA

[ũ] high [+ATR] back rounded nasalized vowel. Occurs word initially in ARA; occurs word medially and finally in all lects.

Word initially

[ũgʷâtà]	'three'	ARA

Word medially

[tsṹŋũ̀]	'bone'	GIR
[bʷòzũgʷó]	'thigh'	GIR
[ɲũgʷózà]	'woman'	GIR, GBB
[ɲũkʷózà]	'woman'	ARA
[nṹwã̀]	'water'	GBB, PAP
[èwũ̂fṹ]	'cotton'	GBB
[sṹkṹ]	'bone'	PAP
[mʲũ̀knũ̀]	'hunger'	ARA

Word finally

[ètsṹ]	'smell'	GIR
[gũ]	'climb'	all
[táfũ]	'fly'	GIR
[sũ̀kṹ]	'bone'	ARA, PAP
[wóʃisṹ]	'hundred'	GBB

[míjasṹ]	'stink'	GBB
[náwṹ]	'extinguish'	PAP
[sṹ]	'swell'	ARA, PAP

Fully specified vowel features matrix

	i	ĩ	ɪ	ɪ̃	e	ẽ	ɛ	ɛ̃	a	ã	ʌ	o	õ	u	ũ	u	ũ
Syllabic/Sonorant/Vd	+	+	+	+	+	+	+	+	+	+	+	+	+	+	+	+	+
Consonantal	−	−	−	−	−	−	−	−	−	−	−	−	−	−	−	−	−
Anterior	+	+	+	+	+	+	+	+	−	−	−	−	−	−	−	−	−
Round	−	−	−	−	−	−	−	−	−	−	−	+	+	−	−	+	+
High	+	+	+	+	−	−	−	−	−	−	−	−	−	+	+	+	+
Back	−	−	−	−	−	−	−	−	+	+	+	+	+	+	+	+	+
Low	−	−	−	−	−	−	−	−	+	+	−	−	−	−	−	−	−
Nasal	−	+	−	+	−	+	−	+	−	+	−	−	+	−	+	−	+
ATR	+	+	−	−	+	+	−	−	−	−	−	+	+	−	−	+	+

2.3 Tones

A phonetic description of the tones and their distribution in specific environments is given below with examples following.

[´]   high tone

    Word initially on vowels

# [e ɛ a ʌ o]		GIR
# [ɛ o]		GBB
# [e ɛ a o]		ARA
# [a ʌ o]		PAP
[áβù]	'meat'	ARA
[ámĩ̀]	'blood'	ARA, PAP
[áɲì]	'soup'	GIR
[áɲìgʷózà]	'female'	GIR
[óbʷa]	'nose'	PAP
[ófù]	'lie'	GBB
[ófʷà]	'farm'	GIR
[ólà]	'sea'	ARA
[ʌ́zò]	'beans'	PAP
[édʲà]	'blood'	GIR
[égʲè]	'sleep'	ARA

Phonetic Description

[ɛ́bè]	'knife'	ARA
[ɛ́bʷà]	'nose'	GBB
[ɛ́ɡ͡bè]	'mouth'	GIR, PAP
[ɛ́knà`]	'thorn'	PAP
[ɛ́tsù]	'king'	GIR
[ʌ́wù]	'thread'	GIR

After voiced obstruents

[b bʲ ɡ͡b d g gʷ ʤ] __		GIR
[b bʷ ɡ͡b ɡ͡bm ɓ g gʷ gʲ ʒ] __		GBB
[b bʷ β βʷ ɡ͡bm ɓ ɓmʲ d dn g gʲ ʒ ʤ] __		ARA
[b ɡ͡b ɡ͡bm ɓ d dn g z ʤ] __		PAP
[èbí]	'child'	GIR, PAP
[èbʲé]	'fat'	GIR
[òdú]	'heart'	GIR, ARA
[ʤà̰]	'wash'	GIR
[gápè]	'jaw'	GIR
[nàgáɡ͡bá]	'crocodile'	GIR
[bʷòzūgʷó]	'thigh'	GIR
[tʃongʷó]	'night'	GIR
[àɡ͡bmí]	'intestine'	ARA
[èɡ͡bmíjà]	'fish'	ARA
[sǎk͡pʌgʲé]	'salt'	ARA
[ùgútnájì]	'six'	ARA
[ʒáβʷì]	'bush'	ARA
[ʃĩɓé]	'descend'	ARA
[ɓmʲǎ]	'good'	ARA
[βǽ]	'all'	ARA
[òβʷá]	'nose'	ARA
[bʌmú]	'palmwine'	ARA
[òbʷá]	'arm'	ARA
[èdná]	'river'	ARA
[ùgʷáwòtʃèàtà]	'thirteen'	PAP
[ɡ͡bmáɲìɡ͡bmî]	'fingernail'	PAP
[dàɡ͡bá]	'elephant'	all
[tsóngʷó]	'night'	GBB
[ʃáʃeʒí]	'sky'	GBB
[bʌɓé]	'breast'	GBB
[lùbá]	'guinea fowl'	GBB

[bídà]	'meat'	GBB
[pítàbʷádà]	'leg'	GBB
[dómʷàɹà]	'mud'	GBB
[èsugʲí]	'king'	GBB
[àgbmí]	'intestine'	GBB
[gĩɹĩ]	'mortar'	GBB
[bʌɓé]	'breast'	PAP
[èbé]	'knife'	PAP
[èdná]	'river'	PAP
[dókʷò]	'horse'	PAP
[àgbámì]	'door'	PAP
[gbéɹè]	'root'	PAP
[ùgútnájì]	'six'	PAP
[èdá]	'father'	ARA
[èdʒé]	'material'	ARA
[ɲĩkʷózá]	'woman'	PAP

After voiceless obstruents

[k͡p p pʲ t tn kʷ s ʃ ts tʃ dʒ n] __		GIR
[k͡p p pʲ k kʷ kɲ f θ s ʃ ts tʃ] __		GBB
[k͡p p tn k kʷ h s ʃ tʃ] __		ARA
[k͡p pʷ pʲ t tn k kʷ hʷ s tʃ] __		PAP

[kɲùk͡pá]	'neck'	GIR
[k͡pàkʷó]	'door'	GIR
[sènʒí]	'sky'	GIR
[èpá]	'urine'	GIR
[pítà]	'foot'	GIR
[èpʲá]	'moon'	GIR, PAP
[ɲàʃá]	'iron'	GIR
[ʃéwò]	'fish'	GIR
[sángʷà]	'grass'	GIR
[èsé]	'wind'	GIR
[osú]	'bee'	GIR
[táfũ]	'fly'	GIR
[túgʷò]	'head'	GIR
[tnâbà]	'seven'	GIR
[kùtʃí]	'fetish'	GIR
[mùtségé]	'mosquito'	GIR
[ʃákʷohí]	'god'	ARA

Phonetic Description

[béjàkó]	'machete'	ARA
[k͡pémà]	'dwell'	ARA
[ʌpá]	'urine'	ARA
[sèsí]	'tail'	ARA
[ùgútnájì]	'six'	ARA
[sètʃé]	'blow'	ARA
[vījùkʷó]	'rainy season'	ARA
[mìntʃĩ]	'saliva'	GBB
[pítàbʷádà]	'leg'	GBB
[èpʲá]	'moon'	GBB
[ʃáʃeʒĩ]	'sky'	GBB
[wóʃĩsũ]	'hundred'	GBB
[fĩtʃéɹé]	'leaf'	GBB
[tsóŋgʷó]	'night'	GBB
[θέθì]	'tail'	GBB
[èwũfũ]	'cotton'	GBB
[búɹèkétʃé]	'dust'	GBB
[kɲík͡pà]	'neck'	GBB
[kàk͡pé]	'basket'	GBB
[k͡pàkʷó]	'door'	GBB
[nàkʷó]	'cow'	PAP
[sìntóló]	'leaf'	PAP
[tseòkũ]	'basket'	PAP
[kàpʷí]	'navel'	PAP
[èpʲá]	'moon'	PAP
[sṹk͡pʌɹè]	'stool'	PAP
[tnâbà]	'seven'	PAP
[òhʷá]	'farm'	PAP
[k͡pásù]	'star'	PAP
[ùgʷáwòtʃéàtà]	'thirteen'	PAP

After sonorants

[wʲ l j m n ɲ ŋ] _		GIR
[w ɹ j m mʷ n ɲ ŋ] _		GBB
[w wʲ l j m n ɲ] _		ARA
[w wʲ ɹ l j m n ɲ e] _		PAP

[láɲugó]	'marry'	GIR
[knṹŋʷẽ]	'six'	GIR
[mátsã̀]	'laugh'	GIR

[emí]	'defecate'	GIR
[ɲǽɓʌɹè]	'root'	GIR
[kʷoɲí]	'sing'	GIR
[ɛnáwù]	'extinguish'	GIR
[pèná]	'roast'	GIR
[wǐgbè]	'thief'	GIR
[βʷìjá]	'spit'	GIR
[èlú]	'bird'	ARA
[gùmá]	'bag'	ARA
[ɓmã̀ɲí]	'one'	ARA
[nǔwã̀]	'water'	ARA
[òwá]	'snake'	ARA
[ewʲí]	'guinea corn'	ARA
[èjá]	'thing'	ARA
[ànú]	'full'	GBB
[nǔwã̀]	'water'	GBB
[ŋáɹèpàɹá]	'jaw'	GBB
[fitʃéɹé]	'leaf'	GBB
[òwá]	'snake'	GBB
[èjá]	'thing'	GBB
[míjasṹ]	'stink'	GBB
[àmʷí]	'dog'	GBB
[ɲíknã̌]	'tooth'	GBB
[lákalà]	'leave'	PAP
[gùmá]	'bag'	PAP
[ɲã́ɲá]	'dance'	PAP
[ɛnú]	'husband'	PAP
[k͡pèɹéɹé]	'round'	PAP
[kã̌wʲí]	'thorn'	PAP
[bʌwú]	'story'	PAP
[ajàknṹ]	'house'	PAP

[ ] mid tone (unmarked). Occurs as follows:

Word initially on vowels

# [e ɛ a o]	GIR
# [ɛ]	GBB
# [e ɛ a ʌ o]	ARA
# [e ɛ a ʌ o]	PAP

Phonetic Description

[adá]	'machete'	GIR
[ajàknṹ]	'house'	ARA, PAP
[ɛdnà]	'fear'	GIR, ARA, PAP
[ɛnáwù]	'extinguish'	GIR
[ɛnú]	'husband'	PAP
[ɛzì]	'palm oil'	GBB
[ʌpá]	'urine'	ARA
[ʌmʷi]	'mosquito'	PAP
[emí]	'defecate'	GIR
[eʤe]	'wine'	ARA
[ejà]	'mother'	PAP
[ewʲí]	'guinea corn'	ARA
[okà]	'snail'	ARA
[ogù]	'fight'	PAP
[osú]	'bee'	GIR, ARA

After voiced obstruents

[ɡ͡bm ɓ g z ʤ] __	GIR
[b g] __	GBB
[b ɓ g v ʒ ʤ] __	ARA
[b ɡ͡b g] __	PAP

[ɡ͡bmɪná]	'feather'	GIR
[ɡ͡bmʲā]	'good'	GIR
[gū]	'climb'	all
[ɲìɓāgʷó]	'old person'	GIR
[wʲeʤiŋɡ͡bmà]	'darkness'	GIR
[zo]	'finish'	GIR
[bʷòzūgʷó]	'thigh'	GIR
[ɛ̀be]	'monkey'	PAP
[ɡ͡baɹì]	'he goat'	PAP
[bináji]	'body'	GBB
[ɛ̀ʒibihí]	'village'	ARA
[kútùɓaɹà]	'turtle'	ARA
[vījùkʷó]	'rainy season'	ARA
[bima]	'give birth'	ARA
[eʤe]	'wine'	ARA

After voiceless obstruents

[k kʷ s tʃ] __	GIR
[k s ʃ] __	GBB
[k͡p p k kʷ] __	ARA
[k͡p t k ts] __	PAP

[si]	'buy'	GIR
[kululu]	'round'	GIR, ARA
[kʷoɲí]	'sing'	GIR
[ɲíkanà]	'buttock'	GIR
[tʃoŋgʷó]	'night'	GIR
[jikala]	'hard'	GIR
[bútukṹ]	'dust'	PAP
[lákalà]	'leave'	PAP
[tseòkṹ]	'basket'	PAP
[sàk͡pʌɹé]	'salt'	PAP
[tunaniʒì]	'think'	PAP
[èsugʲí]	'king'	GBB
[ʃáʃeʒí]	'sky'	GBB
[mùkʌɹé]	'dry season'	GBB, PAP
[petʃè]	'mat'	ARA
[ʃákʷohí]	'god'	ARA
[sàk͡pʌgʲé]	'salt'	ARA
[jákʷonó]	'mother's brother'	ARA
[zòkʷo]	'press'	ARA

After sonorants

[wʲ l j m ɲ] __	GIR
[wʲ l j] __	GBB
[l m] __	ARA
[wʲ l n] __	PAP

[kululu]	'round'	GIR, ARA
[láɲugó]	'marry'	GIR
[mẽ]	'build'	GIR
[mẽ]	'mould'	GIR
[wʲedʒiŋɓmà]	'darkness'	GIR
[jikala]	'hard'	GIR
[binájí]	'body'	GBB
[míjasṹ]	'stink'	GBB

Phonetic Description

[dàwʲe]	'want'	GBB
[wʲi]	'steal'	GBB
[la]	'carry'	GBB
[bima]	'give birth'	ARA
[èwʲi]	'crocodile'	PAP
[la]	'take'	PAP
[mʷàbéɹèlo]	'many'	PAP
[tʊnaniʒì]	'think'	PAP

[`] low tone. Occurs as follows:

Word initially on vowels

# [e ɛ a o]		GIR
# [e ɛ a o]		GBB
# [e ɛ a o u ũ]		ARA
# [e ɛ a o u]		PAP

[àɡ͡bámì]	'door'	PAP
[àmʷí]	'dog'	GBB
[àjíkʷò]	'sing'	PAP
[èdʒé]	'material'	ARA
[èk͡pmì]	'abuse'	GBB
[èpʲá]	'moon'	GIR, GBB, PAP
[èwʲè]	'lizard'	ARA
[èwó]	'money'	GBB
[èbé]	'knife'	PAP
[èbí]	'child'	GIR, PAP
[èdná]	'river'	ARA, PAP
[èmí]	'dew'	GIR, GBB
[èsé]	'wind'	GIR
[ètsṹ]	'smell'	GIR
[èʒibihí]	'village'	ARA
[òβʷá]	'nose'	ARA
[òdú]	'heart'	GIR, ARA
[òɡʷãbà]	'two'	PAP
[òknū]	'war'	GBB, PAP
[ùgútnájì]	'six'	ARA, PAP
[ũgʷâtà]	'three'	ARA
[àɡ͡bmí]	'intestine'	GBB, ARA
[ànú]	'full'	GIR, GBB
[èbʲé]	'fat'	GIR

[èg͡bmíjà]	'fish'	ARA
[èpá]	'urine'	GIR
[èwʲé]	'eye'	all
[èwʲi]	'crocodile'	PAP
[èjá]	'thing'	GBB, ARA
[èbe]	'monkey'	PAP
[èdá]	'father'	GIR, ARA
[èlú]	'bird'	ARA
[èɲí]	'sing'	GBB
[ɛ̀sugʲí]	'king'	GBB
[èwǔfú]	'cotton'	GBB
[ʌmʷi]	'dog'	ARA, PAP
[òbʷá]	'arm'	ARA
[ògǔsīknú]	'fifty'	PAP
[òhʷá]	'farm'	PAP
[òwá]	'snake'	GBB, ARA
[ǔgʷâbà]	'two'	ARA
[ùgʷâwòt͡ʃâtà]	'thirteen'	ARA, PAP

After voiced obstruents

[b bʷ β βʷ g͡b g͡bm ɓ d dʲ dn gʷ gn z] __		GIR
[bʷ g͡b g͡bm d gn z ʒ] __		GBB
[b β βʷ ɓ d dn g gʷ gʲ gn z] __		ARA
[b bʲ β g͡b d dn g gʷ gn z ʒ] __		PAP
[túgʷò]	'head'	GIR
[tnâbà]	'seven'	GIR
[wʲeʤiŋg͡bmà]	'darkness'	GIR
[wʲíg͡bè]	'thief'	GIR
[βʷìjá]	'spit'	GIR
[bʷòzūgʷó]	'thigh'	GIR
[dàg͡bá]	'elephant'	GIR, ARA, PAP
[édʲà]	'blood'	GIR
[ɛdnà]	'fear'	GIR, ARA, PAP
[gnìgwó]	'market'	GIR
[ɲǽɓʌɹè]	'root'	GIR
[ɲǔgʷózà]	'woman'	GIR
[núβòmémè]	'stomach'	GIR
[βàjǽ]	'all'	PAP
[bʌwú]	'story'	PAP

[bʲèíbʲèí]	'red'	PAP
[ɛ́g͡bè]	'mouth'	PAP
[gùmá]	'bag'	PAP
[ʌ́zò]	'beans'	PAP
[dàwʲe]	'want'	GBB
[ɛ́bʷà]	'nose'	GBB
[ɛzì]	'palm oil'	GBB
[g͡bʌ̀ɹi]	'doctor'	GBB
[g͡bmìnθábíɹí]	'stool'	GBB
[gnĩ̀]	'pull'	GBB
[ʒàbúdú]	'waterpot'	GBB
[bʌ̀wú]	'story'	ARA
[égʲè]	'sleep'	ARA
[gìwʲé]	'money'	ARA
[gnĩ̀]	'pull'	ARA
[gʷògʷò]	'hawk'	ARA, PAP
[ʃíɓè]	'medicine'	ARA
[ʒáβʷì]	'bush'	ARA
[zòkʷo]	'press'	ARA
[áβù]	'meat'	ARA
[gnìkʷó]	'market'	PAP
[tunaniʒì]	'think'	PAP

After voiceless obstruents

[k͡p p t k kɲ f fʷ s t͡s] __	GIR
[k͡p k͡pm p t k kn f fʲ θ s ʃ] __	GBB
[t k kʷ kn s ʃ t͡ʃ] __	ARA
[k͡p t k kʷ kn s] __	PAP

[pàtà]	'skin'	GIR
[sɛ̀nʒí]	'sky'	GIR
[táfũ̀]	'fly'	GIR
[ɛ́t͡sù]	'king'	GIR
[kìnú]	'sheep'	GIR
[kɲùk͡pá]	'neck'	GIR
[k͡pàkʷó]	'door'	GIR
[ófʷà]	'farm'	GIR
[dókʷò]	'horse'	ARA
[mʲũ̀knũ̀]	'hunger'	ARA
[músìwʲí]	'cat'	ARA

[okà]	'snail'	ARA
[petʃè]	'mat'	ARA
[ʃĩɓé]	'descend'	ARA
[ùgʷáwòtʃéàtà]	'thirteen'	PAP
[èk͡pmì]	'abuse'	GBB
[θéθì]	'tail'	GBB
[fĩtʃéɹé]	'leaf'	GBB
[p̃ègʷósà]	'dawn'	GBB
[kàk͡pé]	'basket'	GBB
[kɲík͡pà]	'neck'	GBB
[mítàɹà]	'tongue'	GBB
[ʃègʷó]	'rain'	GBB
[k͡pèɹéɹé]	'round'	PAP
[kàpʷí]	'navel'	PAP
[àjĩkʷò]	'sing'	PAP
[ɛ́knà]	'thorn'	PAP
[sũ̀]	'swell'	PAP
[wʲêtò]	'wet'	ARA

After sonorants

[w ɹ j m n ɲ ŋ ŋʷ e] __		GIR
[w wʲ ɹ l j m mʷ n ɲ] __		GBB
[w wʲ ɹ l j m mʲ] __		ARA
[w ɹ l j m mʷ n ɲ e] __		PAP

[tówò]	'thirst'	GIR
[tsúŋù̃]	'bone'	GIR
[áɲì]	'soup'	GIR
[ʤã̀]	'wash'	GIR
[k͡pʌ́jè]	'know'	GIR
[mùtsɛ́gé]	'mosquito'	GIR
[knũŋʷè̃]	'six'	GIR
[ɲæɓʌɹè]	'root'	GIR
[ɲíkanà]	'buttock'	GIR
[èg͡bmíjà]	'fish'	ARA
[èwʲè]	'lizard'	ARA
[k͡pémà]	'dwell'	ARA
[mʲũknũ̀]	'hunger'	ARA
[nũ̀wã̀]	'water'	ARA
[ólà]	'sea'	ARA

Phonetic Description

[kútùɓaɹà]	'turtle'	ARA
[dómʷàɹà]	'mud'	GBB
[èwǔfú]	'cotton'	GBB
[mìntʃǐ]	'saliva'	GBB
[lùbá]	'guinea fowl'	GBB
[ɲákp̂àjì]	'animal'	GBB
[ɲǔgʷózà]	'woman'	GBB
[wʲôwʲò]	'cold'	GBB
[ɡ͡bmínùkǔ]	'fingernail'	GBB
[ámî]	'blood'	PAP
[ɡ͡baɹî]	'he goat'	PAP
[lákalà]	'leave'	PAP
[mʷàbéɹèlo]	'many'	PAP
[ɲìpʲéjì]	'sun'	PAP
[náwǔ]	'extinguish'	PAP
[nàkʷó]	'cow'	PAP
[tseòkú̂]	'basket'	PAP

[ˆ] high falling tone. Does not occur word initially; does occur with obstruents and sonorants as follows.

With voiced obstruents

[gʷ] __		GIR
Does not occur		GBB
[b gʷ] __		ARA
[bʷ ɡ͡bm ӡ] __		PAP

[gʷâbà]	'two'	GIR
[bʷîbʷî]	'white'	PAP
[ɡ͡bmáɲìɡ͡bmî]	'fingernail'	PAP
[bʌ̀mú]	'palm wine'	ARA
[ǔgʷâtà]	'three'	ARA
[ӡîӡî]	'black'	PAP

With voiceless obstruents

[tn] __		GIR
[k] __		GBB
[tʃ] __		ARA
[tn ʃ] __		PAP

[tnâbà]	'seven'	GIR
[ùgʷâwòtʃâtà]	'thirteen'	ARA
[ògúsīknű]	'fifty'	PAP
[kâwé]	'dry'	GBB
[tnâbà]	'seven'	PAP

With sonorants

Does not occur		GIR
[wʲ] __		GBB
[wʲ] __		ARA
[w wʲ] __		PAP
[wʲêtò]	'wet'	ARA
[wʲôwʲò]	'cold'	GBB
[wʲêwò]	'cold'	PAP
[wêwê]	'new'	PAP

[ˇ] low rising tone. Does not occur word initially or with obstruents; occurs with sonorants in ARA.

[l] __

[lǒ] 'enter' ARA

3
Phonological Description

This chapter discusses the basic phonology of Gwari as a whole, and as it exists in each of the lects. The first section (§3.1) is devoted to the phonology of Gwari as a whole, while §§3.2–3.5 discuss each lect individually. Within this framework, §3.1 is generally descriptive, while the following sections introduce specific details as each lect is discussed.

3.1 The phonology of Gwari as a whole

The phonological system of Gwari is noted for the palatal, labial, and nasal modifications allowed for the majority of its consonants. While the individual system of each lect varies somewhat from the others, there is a basic unity which characterizes each as being Gwari.

3.1.1 The syllable structure of Gwari

The phonological system of Gwari is characterized by its complex consonant clusters. The basic syllable structure is (O)(N)(G)V(N), where C = consonant, O = obstruent, N = nasal, G = glide, and V = vowel. There is also a syllabic nasal, and the glide can fill the obstruent slot, producing GGV. The most common syllable type is CV (OV, NV or GV), but ONV and OGV are also very common. ONGV is rare, but does occur. V and N are said to occur as single words, but my data were not extensive enough to give evidence for them. By definition, C includes O, N, and G. The canonic forms for the word patterns are CV, VCV, and CVCV. Neither aspiration nor stress is phonemic. The following syllable structures occur in all of the Gwari lects (examples for each are given later).

CV
CVN
CNV (NNV does not occur)
CGV
CGVN
ONGV

3.1.2 Consonants

Basic consonant phoneme chart for Gwari

		Labial	Alveolar	Palatal	Velar	Labial velar[3]
Plosive	vl.	p	t		k	kp
	vd.	b	d		g	gb
Fricative	vl.	f	s		h	
	vd.	v	z			
Nasal		m	n			
Approximant		l		j		w

Alveopalatals. The full set of alveopalatals are best analyzed as alveolar consonants followed by the palatal glide as shown in the rule below. This allows for a more complete distribution of the palatal glide, and greatly simplifies the phoneme chart. This general rule for alveopalatals has modifications made to it lect specifically. See chapter four for a more complete discussion of the glides.

/Cj/ → [C]
| |
[Alveolar] [Alveopalatal]

Plosives and implosives. Each lect contains a full set of voiced and voiceless plosives. The voiceless plosives are usually slightly aspirated, while the plosion of the voiced ones is generally rather muted, except for the labial velars and the implosive (if it occurs). The voiced labials can be manifested phonetically in a continuum of plosion, i.e., there are [β], [b], [ɡ͡b] and [ɓ]. Phonemically, though, there are usually only two phonemes, /b/ and /gb/; [ɓ] and [ɡ͡b] are either in free variation, or [ɓ] occurs word initially. Southern Gbagyi has /b/, /gb/, and /ɓ/. The voiceless labials also vary in plosion, but not enough that four phones can be distinguished.

---
[3]While [ɓ] occurs in every lect, it is phonemic only in Southern Gbagyi.

Fricatives. While there are a number of phonetic fricatives, generally, only three are phonemes. The Gbagyi lect of GBB has four fricatives, preserving the contrast between [f] and [v]. The labial and velar plosives have fricative allophones which, depending on the lect, are either in free variation or occur word medially in complementary distribution with their plosive counterparts. The alveopalatal fricatives are allophonic with the alveolar fricatives as described above.

Nasals. There are two nasal consonants, /m/ and /n/, which tend to conform in place of articulation to any immediately preceding or following consonant, but there is still evidence of contrast between them, and they both can receive either of the glides (thus there is [mʷ], [mʲ], [ŋʷ] and [ɲ].)

The phonemic syllable structure of /CN.../ is realized differently in various phonetic environments as: /consonant + nasal + vowel/, /postnasalized consonant + vowel/, /consonant + nasalized vowel/, /consonant + nasal + glide/nasalized glide + vowel/, etc. Also, I have taken the position that word-final nasals coalesce with the preceding vowel, thus accounting for word-final nasalized vowels which occur when no other nasal is phonetically present. Nasals can occur then, syllable initially, medially, or finally; /m/ and /n/ contrast syllable initially only, where they also contrast with /b/ and /d/. I have not taken this position dogmatically, but a fuller discussion is found in chapter five.

Liquids. There is some debate over the status of [ɹ] and [l] in Gwari. It is claimed for the Gbagyi lects that [ɹ] exists only rarely outside of borrowed words. It is much more common in Gbari. (Note, for example, their very names). It is my contention that while [ɹ] exists, it is not phonemic, even in Gbari. It is rather, in Gbari, an allophone of [l] such that /lj/→ [ɹ]. This would help to account for the fact that [ɹ] is alveopalatal rather than alveolar, and it does not generally act like a flap. It can sometimes be transcribed [rʲ] as well, and often is a variant with [j] across lects, e.g., /gbàljé/ [gbàlʲé] ~ [gbàɹʲé] 'cat'. While one would perhaps not consider this analysis in other situations, the similar effect of the palatal glide on all other alveolars is striking, while the vowels tend to react to [ɹ] as if it had a palatal glide.

Approximants. The palatal and labial velar approximants occur syllable initially. I have also interpreted the palatalized and labialized consonants as sequences of consonant + approximant (i.e., glide). The approximants contrast in either position. While they have been said to be predictable following consonants, occurring most commonly before vowels with the same value of [back] and [round], they both occur before [a] quite frequently, and, less frequently, before vowels with the opposite feature of [back] and [round]. The reader is referred to §§2.1, 3.(2,3,4,5).2 and chapter four for examples and a fuller discussion of the glide phenomenon.

3.1.3 Vowels

Basic vowel phoneme chart for Gwari

	Front	Central	Back
High	i		u
Mid	e		o
Low		a	

ATR (advanced tongue root). All the lects have [−ATR] allophones of the [−low] vowels occurring word initially and medially. While the rules vary a little from lect to lect, interconsonantal vowels become [−ATR] unless there is a glide on one of the consonants. Word initial vowels also become [−ATR], but the relation between this and the glides is not as clear and the rule is more lect specific.

Assimilation. Vowels tend to assimilate to the following consonant if it is [+high] or to the glide which follows it. This assimilation may not occur, however, if there is a glide preceding the vowel. The presence of a like-featured glide before a vowel strengthens the vowel and helps to prevent it from assimilating. If the vowel does assimilate, the glide preserves the vowel's original features.

Nasality. Nasalization does not appear to be phonemic to the vowels. While they can carry nasalization, they are usually in the company of a nasal when they do so, and they are often not nasalized even then. I believe that the vowel carries the nasality of a nasal consonant when the nasal consonant is in danger of being deleted or assimilated or when this has already occurred. In contrast with Nupe, mid vowels in Gwari can be nasalized, although this occurs very rarely.

3.1.4 Tone

All the literature on Gwari (which is generally in reference to Gbagyi only) agrees that there are three phonemic tones: high /´/, mid / / and low /`/, while phonetically there is also a rising tone [ˆ] and a falling tone [ˇ]. Hyman and Magaji (1970) mention a phonetic lower-mid tone as well, which is mostly morphophonemic. The literature and the Gwari themselves agree

Phonological Description (GIR)   69

that the use of tone varies from lect to lect, the same word carrying a different tone in different lects. While I have been as careful as possible in the transcription of tone for the data I collected, I have not felt confident enough in its accuracy to attempt any analysis of the tonal system at this time. This is due in part to the fact that I am a native speaker of an intonational rather than tonal language, but also to the fact that my transcription of tone did indeed vary from lect to lect on the same words. I hope to thoroughly pursue this aspect of Gwari phonology in the future.

3.2 Southern Gbari (GIR)

3.2.1 Phonetic chart of Southern Gbari

Consonants	Bilabial	Labio-dental	Alveolar	Alveo-palatal	Palatal	Velar	Labial velar
Plain consonants							
Plosive	p		t	tʃ		k	k͡p
	b		d	dʒ		g	g͡b
Implosive	ɓ						
Fricative		f	s	ʃ		h	
	β		z	ʒ			
Affricate			ts				
Nasal	m		n	ɲ		ŋ	
Approximant			l	ɹ	j		w
Labialized consonants							
Plosive	pʷ					kʷ	k͡pʷ
	bʷ					gʷ	
Implosive	ɓʷ						
Fricative		fʷ					
	βʷ						
Nasal	mʷ					ŋʷ	
Palatalized consonants							
Plosive	pʲ		tʲ			kʲ	
	bʲ		dʲ			gʲ	
Fricative	ɸʲ	fʲ					
Nasal	mʲ						
Approximant				ɹʲ			wʲ

Vowels		Front	Central	Back
High	[+ATR]	i ĩ		u ũ
	[−ATR]	ɪ ĩ		ʊ ʊ̃
Mid	[+ATR]	e ẽ		o õ
	[−ATR]	ɛ ɛ̃		ʌ
Low			a ã	

3.2.2 Evidence of contrast

p/k͡p
[pátà]   'skin'
[k͡pátʃĩ]   'cough'

b/g͡b
[βèβè]   'whistle'
[ɓɛ́ɓɛ́]   'breast'

t/d
[tówò]   'thirst'
[dógʷò]   'horse'

k/k͡p
[kàté]   'room'
[k͡pátʃĩ]   'cough'

f/s
[fù]   'wash'
[sũ̀]   'make'

j/w
[jágʷò]   'maternal uncle'
[wá]   'ask'

j/l
[jánũ̀wã́]   'swim'
[láɲugʷó]   'marry'

i/e
[gʲì]   'beat (drum)'
[gʲè]   'see'

e/o
[èβʷé]   'play'
[òβʷé]   'calabash'

p/b
[pà]   'tie'
[bà]   'lose'

k͡p/g͡b
[k͡pmà]   'take off'
[g͡bmíjà]   'surpass'
[k͡pàkʷó]   'door'
[g͡bakʷòkʷò] 'cloud'

k/g
[kàk͡pé]   'basket'
[gápɛ̀]   'jaw'

g/g͡b
[ɓámà]   'plantain'
[gánà]   'jump'
[g͡bmájà]   'break'
[gnádo]   'split'

s/z
[si]   'buy'
[zìjá]   'pour'

m/n
[màgʷé]   'sister'
[nàgʷò]   'cow'

u/o
[dò]   'enter'
[dù]   'cook'

i/u
[sĩ]   'swell'
[sũ̀]   'make'

high/mid/low tone

[ɛmí]	'defecate'	[kná]	'send'
[èmí]	'oil'	[kna]	'fry'
[éɲì]	'soup'	[jé]	'like'
[èɲí]	'song'	[je]	'suck'
		[jè]	'reply'

3.2.3 Evidence of syllable structure

CV	/bà/ 'count', /wá/ 'ask', /mi/ 'swallow'
CVN	/bòntí/ 'banana', /mìntí/ 'saliva'
CGV	/bwò/ 'rotten', /wjí/ 'steal', /ŋwà/ 'catch'
CGVN/CGNV	/tjínkpè/ /tjníkpè/ 'stool'
CNV/CVN	/kná/ 'send', /jnàsja/ /jànsja/ 'iron'
ONGV	/gbnja/ 'good', /èknjí/ 'ground'

3.2.4 Rules

The following rules apply.

Nasal assimilation. An alveolar nasal becomes a velar nasal when followed by a [+back] consonant, and a bilabial nasal when preceded or followed by a labial consonant. This is seen in [t͡ʃíŋk͡pè] /tjínkpè/ 'stool', [kàmbá] /kànbá/ 'maize', and [g͡bmínà] /gbnínà/ 'feather'.

$$\begin{bmatrix} +\text{consonantal} \\ +\text{nasal} \end{bmatrix} \rightarrow \begin{matrix} [+\text{back}] \\ \\ [+\text{labial}] \end{matrix} \Big/ \begin{matrix} \_\_ \begin{bmatrix} +\text{consonantal} \\ +\text{back} \end{bmatrix} \\ \\ \_\_ \begin{bmatrix} +\text{consonantal} \\ +\text{labial} \end{bmatrix} \end{matrix}$$

Vowel nasality assimilation. A vowel may become nasalized in the environment of a nasal consonant, e.g., [t͡ʃìkná̃] /tjìkná/ 'bush' and [g̃íni] /gjíni/ 'mortar'; but also [zàŋʷé] /zàngwé/ 'human'. If the nasal consonant occurs word finally, the rule is obligatory. This rule must be ordered before the following rule which deletes word final nasal consonants since nasal consonants never occur word finally on the surface level. (See chapter five for a fuller discussion of this.)

$$[+\text{syllabic}] \rightarrow [+\text{nasal}] \: / \: \underline{} \begin{bmatrix} +\text{consonantal} \\ +\text{nasal} \end{bmatrix} \#$$

$$/ \begin{bmatrix} +\text{consonantal} \\ +\text{nasal} \end{bmatrix} \text{(optional)}$$

Nasal consonant deletion rule. Combined, the two previous rules actually describe a process of nasal coalescence. A coalescence rule, however, would not have the flexibility of description which the combined two rules have, especially given the optionality of their application. Nasal consonants often coalesce with the vowel preceding or following them. If they are word final this coalescence is obligatory and results in a word-final nasalized vowel. Word-medial nasals do not have to conform to this rule, but they often do: /sjìn/ [ʃĩ] 'descend', /bwándjè/ [bʷã́ʤè] 'right(side)', and /tjongwó/ [tsõngʷo] 'night'.

$$\begin{bmatrix} +\text{consonantal} \\ +\text{nasal} \end{bmatrix} \rightarrow \begin{matrix} \emptyset & / \: \tilde{V} \underline{} \# \\ \emptyset & / \: \tilde{V} \end{matrix} \quad \text{(optional)}$$

Syllable internal nasals also coalesce, but in different ways depending upon the manner of articulation of the preceding consonant. The ambivalence of the above rules reflects this. When the nasal follows a plosive, the vowel may or may not be nasalized, and the plosive is usually postnasalized. Before [+high] vowels, sometimes only the vowel is nasalized. If the nasal follows another type of consonant only the vowel is nasalized, which sometimes makes it hard to distinguish from CVN: /dná/ [dna] 'dwell', /gní/ [gnĩ́] 'pull', and /snágwò/ [ságʷò] 'grass'.

On voiced labials. The voiced bilabial plosive [b] is very soft and is in free variation with [β]. This is in contrast with the voiced labial velar plosive [g͡b] which always retains its plosion and is an allophone of [ɓ], and occurs when followed by a nasal (which is always [m]). Although [ɓ] is the more common phone, I chose to represent the phoneme as /gb/, thus pairing it with /kp/ which never loses it's plosion: /bébè/ [βéβè] 'whistle', /bètá/ [bètá] 'word', /dàgbá/ [dàɓá] 'elephant', /dágbmá/ [dág͡bmá] 'older brother'.

Phonological Description (GIR) 73

/b/ → [β] (optional)
/gb/ → [ɡ͡b] / __ N
       [ɓ] / elsewhere

Coalescence rule for labialization. Any sequence of consonant plus labial velar glide is realized phonetically as a labialized consonant: /kwankwàsa/ [kʷankʷàsa] 'kite'. A generative rule is given here also where SD indicates structural description and SC structural change.

```
    C    w    V    →    [Cʷ         V]
    1    2    3         1      ∅    3
SD:      1    2    3
SC:      1    ∅    3
         |
    [+round]
```

Coalescence rule for palatalization. Any sequence of [−coronal] consonant plus palatal glide is realized phonetically as a palatalized consonant: /jèmpjé/ [jèmpʲé] 'feces'.

$$\begin{bmatrix} /pj/ \\ /kj/ \\ /bj/ \\ /gj/ \\ /fj/ \\ /mj/ \\ /wj/ \end{bmatrix} \rightarrow \begin{bmatrix} [pʲ] \\ [kʲ] \\ [bʲ] \\ [gʲ] \\ [fʲ] \\ [mʲ] \\ [wʲ] \end{bmatrix}$$

When a palatal glide follows certain alveolar consonants as listed in the next rule, the sequence is realized phonetically as an alveopalatal consonant; /dj/ and /lj/ have some varying phonetic forms. Compare /èdjé/ [èdʲé] 'cloth', /gbadjìdjì/ [ɓadʒìdʒì] 'cloud', /gbàljé/ [ɡ͡bàlʲé] ~ [ɡ͡bàɹʲé] ~ [ɡ͡bàɹé] 'cat', and /tjásjè/ [tʃáʃè] 'God'.

$$\begin{bmatrix} /sj/ \\ /zj/ \\ /nj/ \end{bmatrix} \rightarrow \begin{bmatrix} [ʃ] \\ [ʒ] \\ [ɲ] \end{bmatrix}$$

/dj/ → [dʒ] ~ [dʲ]
/lj/ → [ɹʲ] ~ [ɹ]   (optional)

The sequence /tj/ can be manifested phonetically as [tʲ], [tʃ] or [ts], as shown below, depending upon the following vowel; [tʲ] and [tʃ] are in free variation. [ts] is treated as a realization of /tj/ because the same words in other dialects have the phone [tʃ] instead and there is a very limited distribution of [ts]. There is only one example of it receiving any modifications, as in /tjújà/ 'to push (something)' which can be either [tsújà] or [tsʷíjà].

There is no reason to posit a double obstruent syllable structure and this example is too weak to force a recognition of [ts] as a phoneme, especially as the action of the [ʷ] can be used instead to illustrate the protective function of the glide. [ʷ] is clearly seen to be preserving the values of [+back] and [+round] in a [−round] environment: /tjímwà/ [tʃímʷà] 'firewood', /ètjú/ [ètsú] 'rat'.

/tj/ → [tʲ] ~ [tʃ]   V / __ [−round]
      [ts]   V / __ [+round]

On [r] and [l]. The only example of [ɹ] initially is in the Hausa loan word 'cassava' [ɹógʷò]. It seems better therefore, to posit [ɹ] as an allophone of [l], thus completing the alveolar to alveopalatal pattern. This reasoning is further substantiated by the free fluctuation of [lʲ], [ɹʲ] and [ɹ] exemplified in the rule above.

Vowel feature assimilation. The [−low] vowels tend to assimilate to the following consonant when there is no preceding consonant with the same value of [back] as the vowel, and the following C is [+high] as in /dùjá/ [dìjá] 'pass by'.

$$\begin{bmatrix} +\text{syllabic} \\ -\text{low} \\ \alpha\text{back} \end{bmatrix} \rightarrow [-\alpha\text{back}] \Bigg/ \left(\begin{bmatrix} -\text{syllabic} \\ -\alpha\text{back} \end{bmatrix}\right) \underline{\quad} \begin{bmatrix} -\text{syllabic} \\ +\text{high} \\ -\alpha\text{back} \end{bmatrix}$$

It should be noted in the situation given in the next rule that the values of [back] and [round] are in free fluctuation and the phonemic status of the vowel is in question: /njùgwó/ ~ /njìgwó/ [ɲùgʷo] ~ [ɲìgʷo] 'wife'.

G   V   C   G
[αback]   [−αback]

On ATR. The [+ATR] vowels become [-ATR] when they are word medial and there is no glide of the same value of [back] in the same or following syllable as in /bolófwà/ [bʌlófʷà] 'robe', /gbégbé/ [ɓɛ́ɓé] 'breast'.

$$\begin{bmatrix} V \\ +ATR \\ \alpha back \end{bmatrix} \rightarrow [-ATR] / \begin{pmatrix} C & G \\ & [-\alpha back] \end{pmatrix} \_\_\_ \begin{pmatrix} C & G \\ & [-\alpha back] \end{pmatrix}$$

Word initial vowels may follow the rule which is common to the other lects in one form or another, and says that word initial vowels become [-ATR] when they are followed by a [-high] consonant without a glide, but their [ATR] value is actually in free variation: /òdu/ [òdú] or [ʌ̀dú] 'heart'.

$$\begin{bmatrix} +syllabic \\ +ATR \end{bmatrix} \rightarrow [-ATR] \ / \ \# \_\_\_ \begin{bmatrix} -syllabic \\ -high \end{bmatrix} \begin{bmatrix} -syllabic \\ -high \end{bmatrix}$$

3.2.5 Phoneme chart of Southern Gbari

Consonants		Labial	Alveolar	Palatal	Velar	Labial velar
Plosive	vl.	p	t		k	kp
	vd.	b	d		g	gb
Fricative	vl.	f	s			
	vd.		z			
Nasal		m	n			
Approximant			l	j		w

Vowels	Front	Central	Back
High	i		u
Mid	e		o
Low		a	

3.3 Northern Gbari (GBB)

3.3.1 Phonetic chart of Northern Gbari

Consonants	Bilabial	Labio-dental	Inter-dental	Alveolar	Alveo-palatal	Palatal	Velar	Labial velar
Plain consonants								
Plosive	p			t	tʃ		k	k͡p
	b			d	ʤ		g	g͡b
Implosive	ɓ							
Fricative		f	θ	s	ʃ			
	β			z	ʒ		ɣ	
Nasal	m			n	ɲ		ŋ	
Approximant				l	ɹ	j		w
Labialized consonants								
Plosive	pʷ						kʷ	k͡bʷ
	bʷ						gʷ	g͡bʷ
Fricative		fʷ		sʷ	βʷ			
Nasal	mʷ							
Palatalized consonants								
Plosive	pʲ							
	bʲ			dʲ			gʲ	
Fricative		fʲ						
Nasal	mʲ							
Approximant								wʲ

Vowels		Front	Central	Back
High	[+ATR]	i ĩ		u ũ
	[−ATR]	ɪ		ʊ ʊ̃
Mid	[+ATR]	e		o õ
	[−ATR]	ɛ		ʌ ʌ̃
Low			a ã	

3.3.2 Evidence of contrast

p/k͡p

[páʃè]	'to urinate'		[pàtá]	'skin'
[k͡pàzédʲè]	'friend'		[bàɹé]	'cat'
[èpá]	'urine'		[pèná]	'to roast'
[ʌk͡pmá]	'press'		[bètá]	'word'

p/b

b/g͡b

			[pítàbʷádà]	'foot'
[bàɹé]	'cat'		[bídà]	'meat'
[g͡bʌɹí]	'doctor'			

Phonological Description (GBB)

[bʌbè]	'breast'		k͡p/g͡b
[ʌg͡bé]	'mouth'	[k͡pákù]	'tortoise'
t/d		[g͡bákù]	'axe'
[tókʷòjí]	'short'		k/g
[dókʷò]	'horse'	[kùɹí]	'round'
tʃ/dʒ		[gúdò]	'to bark'
[tʃĩ]	'to sew'	[múkʌɹé]	'dry season'
[dʒì]	'to give'	[ògú]	'fight'
k/k͡p			g/g͡b
[kàk͡pé]	'basket'	[gádà]	'machete'
[k͡pákù]	'tortoise'	[g͡báɹà]	'leopard'
[dàkájì]	'junior brother'	[dàg͡bá]	'elephant'
f/s			s/z
[fì]	'to sweep'	[sù]	'to die'
[θì] ~ [sì]	'to arrive'	[zúgʷo]	'hoe'
[fù]	'to wash (body)'		j/w
[sù]	'to die'	[èjá]	'thing'
m/n		[òwá]	'rope'
[múkʌɹé]	'dry season'	[jàná]	'grass'
[núg͡bàjí]	'male'	[ŋʷa]	'to catch'
j/ɹ		[bʲà]	'to blow'
[bɪnájì]	'body'	[bʷa]	'to count'
[kɲàɹí]	'red'	[mʲūkũ̀]	'hunger'
[mʷàjá]	'request'	[kapʷí]	'crab'
[mʷàɹí]	'horn'	[zàmʷí]	'forget'
[domʷàɹà]	'mud'		w/wʲ
ɹ/l		[kâwé]	'dry'
[gúlú]	'tree bark'	[dàwʲé]	'want'
[kʊkúɹù]	'knee'		
i/e			u/o
[ʃĩ]	'look for'	[wù]	'kill'
[ʃè]	'throw'	[wò]	'hear'
[gʲì]	'beat (drum)'		
[gʲè]	'see'		e/o
i/u		[èwʲé]	'eye'
[ásĩ]	'swell'	[kâwé]	'dry'
[ésũ]	'smell'	[èwó]	'money'
	high/mid/low tone		
[k͡pé]	'to open'	[k͡pe]	'to know'
[k͡pè]	'to remember'		

3.3.3 Evidence of syllable structure

N	/ǹwá/ 'need'
CV	/pò/ 'wash', /nàgwó/ 'cow', /wò/ 'to hear'
CVN	/kànbá/ 'maize'
CGV	/bwá/ 'to play', /mwákpà/ 'tall', /wjì/ 'steal'
CGVN	/kàtjémpà/ 'wall'
CNV	/gnà/ 'to divide', /jníknà/ 'tooth', (no NNV)
ONGV	/gbmjá/ 'good', /knjíkpà/ 'neck', /èknjí/ 'earth'

3.3.4 Rules

The following rules apply.

Nasal assimilation. An alveolar nasal becomes a velar nasal when followed by a [+back] consonant as /ǹwá/ [ŋ̀wá] 'to need'. It becomes a labial nasal in the environment of a labial consonant: /kànbá/ [kàmbá] 'maize' and /gbwágbnà/ [gbʷágbmà] 'arm'. The labial nasal does not assimilate, /àmwí/ [àmʷí] 'dog'.

$$\begin{bmatrix} +\text{nasal} \\ -\text{labial} \end{bmatrix} \rightarrow \begin{array}{l} [+\text{back}] \quad / \underline{\quad} \begin{bmatrix} +\text{syllabic} \\ +\text{back} \end{bmatrix} \\ \\ [+\text{labial}] \quad / \underline{\quad} \begin{bmatrix} +\text{syllabic} \\ +\text{labial} \end{bmatrix} \end{array}$$

Nasal assimilation on vowels. A vowel may become nasalized in the environment of a nasal: /èmí/ [èmĩ́] 'dew', /knúknù/ [knúknũ̀] 'mountain', but also /músànà/ [múθãnà] 'sand'.

$$[+\text{syllabic}] \rightarrow [+\text{nasal}] \quad / \text{ nasal (optional)}$$

Consonant softening. The voiced labial and velar plosives soften to fricatives word medially when followed by a glide: /knúbʷà/ [knúβʷà] 'ear' and /bwózùgwó/ [bʷózùɣʷó] 'thigh'. Although the alveolar plosive plus glide is not included in this rule, it is also realized differently word medially as opposed to word initially. (See the discussion under coalescence rule for palatalization below.)

$$\begin{bmatrix} b \\ g \end{bmatrix} \rightarrow \begin{bmatrix} \beta \\ \gamma \end{bmatrix} / \begin{Bmatrix} V \\ N \end{Bmatrix} \_ G$$

Coalescence rule for labialization. Any consonant glide sequences coalesce to become a labialized consonant as in /dómwàɹà/ [dómʷàɹà] 'mud'.

/Cw/ → [Cʷ]

Coalescence rule for palatalization. A [−coronal] consonant, when followed by the palatal glide, coalesces with the glide to form a palatalized consonant as in /èsugjí/ [èsugʲí] 'king'.

$$\begin{bmatrix} /pj/ \\ /bj/ \\ /gj/ \\ /mj/ \\ /wj/ \end{bmatrix} \rightarrow \begin{bmatrix} [pʲ] \\ [bʲ] \\ [gʲ] \\ [mʲ] \\ [wʲ] \end{bmatrix}$$

When a palatal glide follows an alveolar consonant, the cluster is realized phonetically as an alveopalatal consonant such that /tjàbwá/ 'needle' is realized as [tʃàβʷá], and /gjèsjèná/ 'mat' is realized as [gʲèʃèná]. The glide /dj/ differs slightly in that it only changes to [ʤ] word initially as in /djì/ [ʤi] 'give', and remains [dʲ] word medially as in /èdjé/ [èdʲé] 'wine'. See consonant softening above which illustrates a similar phenomenon with the other voiced plosives.

$$\begin{bmatrix} /tj/ \\ /sj/ \\ /zj/ \\ /nj/ \end{bmatrix} \rightarrow \begin{bmatrix} [tʃ] \\ [ʃ] \\ [ʒ] \\ [ɲ] \end{bmatrix}$$

/dj/ → [ʤ] / # _

On the status of [θ]. The phoneme /s/ is in free variation with [θ] when it is not followed by a glide. I originally thought [θ] to be the result of a speech impediment of a particular language helper, but work in other Northern Gbari villages confirmed its existence. It is an example of the fragmentation of the lects, and is used inconsistently as a mark of distinction from other lects.

As it occurs mainly with front vowels, it is possible that it is used to differentiate /s/ from /sj/ which can be hard to distinguish in that environment. There are examples of it occurring with [a], as in [mínθà] ~ [mínsà] 'man', but it does not occur phonemically with any other [+back] vowel.

/s/ → [θ] / __ V (optional)

Vowel feature assimilation. The [−low] vowels assimilate to the following consonant when there is no preceding glide and the following consonant is [+high] as in [túkʷò] 'head'.

$$\begin{bmatrix} -\text{low} \\ \alpha\text{round} \\ \alpha\text{back} \end{bmatrix} \rightarrow \begin{bmatrix} -\alpha\text{round} \\ -\alpha\text{back} \end{bmatrix} / \begin{bmatrix} -\text{syllabic} \\ -\text{high} \end{bmatrix} \_\_ \left\{ \begin{bmatrix} -\text{syllabic} \\ +\text{high} \\ \begin{bmatrix} -\alpha\text{round} \\ -\alpha\text{back} \end{bmatrix} \end{bmatrix} \right\}$$

On ATR. The [+ATR] vowels become [−ATR] when they are followed by a consonant which does not have a glide or the glide is not of the same value of [back] and there is no glide preceding them as in /mítàɹà/ [mítàɹà] 'tongue', /kukuɹí/ [kʊkʊɹí] 'all' and /ògbé/ [ʌɡ́bé] 'mouth'.

$$\begin{matrix} +\text{ATR} \\ \alpha\text{round} \end{matrix} \rightarrow [-\text{ATR}] / \left(\begin{bmatrix} -\text{syllabic} \\ -\text{high} \end{bmatrix} \right) \_\_ \left\{ \begin{bmatrix} -\text{syllabic} \\ -\text{high} \\ \begin{bmatrix} +\text{high} \\ -\alpha\text{round} \end{bmatrix} \end{bmatrix} \right\}$$

3.3.5 Phoneme chart of Northern Gbari

Consonants		Labial	Alveolar	Palatal	Velar	Labial velar
Plosive	vl.	p	t		k	kp
	vd.	b	d		g	gb
Fricative	vl.	f	s			
	vd.		z			
Nasal		m	n			
Approximant			l/ɹ	j		w

Phonological Description (ARA)

Vowels	Front	Central	Back
High	i		u
Mid	e		o
Low		a	

3.4 Southern Gbagyi (ARA)

3.4.1 Phonetic chart of Southern Gbagyi

Consonants	Bilabial	Labio-dental	Alveolar	Alveo-palatal	Palatal	Velar	Glottal	Labial velar
Plain consonants								
Plosive	p		t	tʃ		k		kp
	b		d	dʒ		g		gb
Implosive	ɓ							
Fricative	ɸ	f	s	ʃ			h	
	β		z	ʒ				
Nasal	m		n	ɲ		ŋ		
Approximant			l		j			w
Labialized consonants								
Plosive						k^w		
	b^w					g^w		gb^w
Fricative		f^w						
	$β^w$							
Nasal	m^w					$ŋ^w$		
Palatalized consonants								
Plosive	p^j							
	b^j					g^j		
Fricative		f^j						
Nasal	m^j							
Approximant								w^j

Vowels		Front	Central	Back
High	[+ATR]	i ĩ		u ũ
	[−ATR]	ɪ		ʊ ʊ̃
Mid	[+ATR]	e		o õ
	[−ATR]	ɛ		ʌ
Low			a ã	

3.4.2 Evidence of contrast

	p/k͡p			p/b	
[petʃè]		'mat'	[pítà]		'foot'
[k͡péjè]		'know'	[bímà]		'give birth'
	b/ɓ			k͡p/g͡b	
[ɓèjá̃]		'ask'	[k͡pmà]		'take off'
[béjàkʷó]		'machete'	[g͡bmá]		'swim'
	k/k͡p			g/g͡b	
[káʃì]		'arrive'	[gʊ̀lù]		'vulture'
[k͡pásù]		'star'	[g͡búk͡pùgʲè]		'chin'
	t/d			k/g	
[tòwò]		'taste'	[kàlá]		'strong'
[dókʷo]		'horse'	[gà]		'give'
	f/s			v/z	
[fĩ̀]		'sweep'	[vʲí]		'follow'
[sĩ̀]		'drink'	[ʒì]		'return'
	f/v			s/z	
[fĩ̀]		'sweep'	[súkʷò]		'night'
[vĩ́júkʷò]		'rainy season'	[zúkʷò]		'hoe'
	m/n			l/n	
[mʊkʊ̀gʲé]		'dry season'	[lákà]		'stand up'
[núkʷòhí]		'bad'	[náknã̀]		'charcoal'
	j/w			w/wʲ	
[àjé]		'liver'	[káwè]		'dry'
[káwè]		'dry'	[knàwʲi]		'arrow'
	i/e			u/o	
[ájì]		'call'	[wú]		'show'
[àjé]		'liver'	[wò]		'hear'
	i/u			e/o	
[sĩ̀]		'drink'	[kàwé]		'dry'
[sũ̀]		'swell'	[wò]		'hear'
		high/mid/low tone			
[jí]		'dig'	[èwʲè]		'lizard'
[jĩ̀]		'lick'	[èwʲé]		'eye'
			[ewʲí]		'guinea corn'

3.4.3 Evidence of syllable structure

N	/ǹtúknjìbéjà/ 'why'
CV	/dà/ 'say', /mí/ 'swallow', /jé/ 'want'
CNV	/gna/ 'divide', /jnítàlà/ 'tongue', (no NNV)
CGV	/gjè/ 'scratch', /mwákpà/ 'long', /wji/ 'steal'
ONGV	/ègbnjá/ 'fish', /knji/ 'choose'

3.4.4 Rules

The following rules apply.

Nasal assimilation. The nasal becomes a velar nasal when followed by a [+back] consonant, and becomes a labial nasal when preceded by a [+labial] consonant. This is seen in [ʃíŋwà] 'tree', [gbmínà] 'feather', and (by exclusion) [mʷàjí] 'horn'.

$$[+\text{nasal}] \rightarrow \begin{matrix} [+\text{back}] \\ [+\text{labial}] \end{matrix} \quad / \quad \begin{matrix} \underline{\quad} \begin{bmatrix} -\text{syllabic} \\ +\text{back} \end{bmatrix} \\ [+\text{labial}] \underline{\quad} \end{matrix}$$

Vowel nasalization. Vowels may become nasalized in the environment of a nasal, as in [nágbmã] /nágbna/ 'older brother'.

$$[+\text{syllabic}] \rightarrow [+\text{nasal}] \quad / \text{ nasal (optional)}$$

Coalescence rule for nasals. In a sequence of consonant plus nasal plus vowel, the nasal may coalesce with the vowel, producing a CV structure. The plosives generally become postnasalized, while the vowel following a postnasalized consonant may or may not be nasalized; [k] frequently does not become postnasalized, [àkní] ~ [àkĩ] 'saliva'.

```
     C    N    V         [C⁽ⁿ⁾         Ṽ]
     1    2    3          1      ∅     3    (optional)
SD:  1    2    3
SC:  1    ∅    3
     |
   [+nasal]
```

On voiced labials. The voiced bilabial plosive is in free variation with the voiced bilabial fricative.

/b/ → [β]   (optional)

[g͡b] is in free variation with [ɓ]; [ɓ] is a little more implosive than [g͡b], but this appears to be the only real difference between the two. Also, /gb/ is in contrast with /b/ which has [β] as an allophone.

/gb/ → [ɓ]   (optional)

Coalescence rule for labialization. Every consonant plus labial glide swquence becomes a labialized consonant, e.g., /mápwí/ [máp^{w}í] 'sister'.

```
    C   w   V    →    [C^w       V]
    1   2   3         1      ∅    3
SD: 1   2   3
SC: 1   ∅   3
    |
  [+round]
```

Coalescence rule for palatalization. The phonetic realization of the alveolars (except /l/) followed by a palatal glide is as alveopalatals; /l/ is not followed by a palatal glide in this lect. (Nor does this lect have [ɹ], except in loan words.) /djàmwúnjì/ [d͡ʒàm^{w}úɲì] 'orange'.

$$\begin{bmatrix} /tj/ \\ /dj/ \\ /sj/ \\ /zj/ \\ /nj/ \end{bmatrix} \rightarrow \begin{bmatrix} [t\!ʃ] \\ [d\!ʒ] \\ [ʃ] \\ [ʒ] \\ [ɲ] \end{bmatrix}$$

When a nonalveolar consonant is followed by the palatal glide, the sequence is realized as a palatalized consonant, /èpjá/ [èp^{j}á] 'moon'.

```
     C     j   V   →   [C^j   V]
[−coronal]
```

On /j/ and /h/. [h] is in free variation with [j] when [j] occurs before [i] in the last syllable of a word. It appears to be merely a loss of voicing in this situation, but PAP apparently has /h/ as an allophone with /f/. It is possible that [h] occurs in other situations in ARA as well, but it does not occur in my data. /njìpjéji/ [ɲìp^{j}éhí] ~ [ɲìp^{j}éjí] 'day'.

/j/ → [h] / __ i# (optional)

Vowel feature assimilation. The [−low] vowels assimilate to the following consonant when there is no preceding glide and the following consonant is [+high] or labialized. In this rule, it is often impossible to recognize the original vowel. Rather, the phenomenon is that [+high] or labialized consonants always force the vowel to assimilate unless there is a preceding glide. Sometimes, even then, the assimilation takes place with the glide being the only evidence of the former vowel: [k͡péjè] /kpéjè/ or /kpójè/ 'know', [ɲíkùtúkʷò] /njíkùtúkwò/ or /njikùtíkwo/ 'knee'.

$$\begin{bmatrix} +\text{syllabic} \\ -\text{low} \\ \alpha\text{back} \\ \alpha\text{round} \end{bmatrix} \rightarrow \begin{bmatrix} -\alpha\text{back} \\ -\alpha\text{round} \end{bmatrix} / \begin{bmatrix} -\text{syllabic} \\ -\text{consonantal} \end{bmatrix} \_\_ \begin{bmatrix} [-\text{syllabic}] \\ \left\{ \begin{bmatrix} +\text{high} \end{bmatrix} \atop \begin{bmatrix} -\alpha\text{back} \\ -\alpha\text{round} \end{bmatrix} \right\} \end{bmatrix}$$

On ATR. Word initially, [+ATR] vowels become [−ATR] when the following consonant is [−high] or [−round] as in [òβʷá] 'nose', [òk͡pmí] 'okra', and [ʌdú] 'heart'.

$$[+\text{ATR}] \rightarrow [-\text{ATR}] \ / \ \# \_\_ \begin{bmatrix} [-\text{syllabic}] \\ \left\{ \begin{matrix} [-\text{round}] \\ [-\text{high}] \end{matrix} \right\} \end{bmatrix}$$

The [+ATR] vowels become [−ATR] when they are word medial and there is no glide of the same value of [back] preceding or following them, as in [ʃík͡pʌgìè] /sjínkpògjè/ 'stool' and [bùzùkʷó] /bùzùkwó/ 'housefly'.

$$\begin{bmatrix} +\text{syllabic} \\ \alpha\text{back} \\ \alpha\text{round} \\ +\text{ATR} \end{bmatrix} \rightarrow [-\text{ATR}] \ / \ \begin{bmatrix} -\text{syllabic} \\ -\text{high} \\ -\alpha\text{back} \\ -\alpha\text{round} \end{bmatrix} \begin{bmatrix} [-\text{syllabic}] \\ \left\{ \begin{bmatrix} -\text{high} \end{bmatrix} \atop \begin{bmatrix} -\alpha\text{back} \\ -\alpha\text{round} \end{bmatrix} \right\} \end{bmatrix}$$

3.4.5 Phoneme chart of Southern Gbagyi

Consonants		Labial	Alveolar	Palatal	Velar	Labial velar
Plosive	vl.	p	t		k	kp
	vd.	b	d		g	gb
Fricative	vl.	f	s			
	vd.	v	z			
Nasal		m	n			
Approximant			l	j		w

Vowels	Front	Central	Back
High	i		u
Mid	e		o
Low		a	

3.5 Northern Gbagyi (PAP)

3.5.1 Phonetic chart of Northern Gbagyi

Consonants	Bilabial	Labio-dental	Alveolar	Alveo-palatal	Palatal	Velar	Glottal	Labial velar
Plain consonants								
Plosive	p		t	tʃ		k		k͡p
	b		d	dʒ		g		g͡b
Implosive	ɓ							
Fricative			s	ʃ			h	
			z	ʒ				
Nasal	m		n	ɲ		ŋ		
Approximant			l	ɹ	j			w
Labialized consonants								
Plosive	pʷ					kʷ		k͡bʷ
	bʷ					gʷ		g͡bʷ
Fricative		fʷ					hʷ	
	βʷ	vʷ				ɣʷ		
Nasal	mʷ					ŋʷ		
Palatalized consonants								
Plosive	pʲ					gʲ		
	bʲ		dʲ					
Fricative		fʲ				ɣʲ		
Nasal	mʲ							
Approximant								wʲ

Phonological Description (PAP)

Vowels		Front	Central	Back
High	[+ATR]	i ĩ		u ũ
	[−ATR]	ɪ		ʊ
Mid	[+ATR]	e		o
	[−ATR]	ɛ		ʌ
Low			a ã	

3.5.2 Evidence of contrast

p/k͡p
[pà] 'tie'
[k͡pà] 'remember'

b/g͡b
[bà] 'pay'
[ɓà] 'break'
[g͡bʷálàg͡bʷálà] 'warm'
[bʷádà] 'hand'

t/d
[tájí] 'bow'
[dà] 'say'

k/k͡p
[knà] 'fry'
[k͡pmá] 'take off'

s/z
[ʌsú] 'bee'
[ʌ́zù] 'housefly'

s/f
[ʃè] 'spin'
[fʲe] 'you pl'

i/e
[èwʲí] 'crocodile'
[èwʲé] 'lizard'

e/o
[lò] 'enter'
[lù] 'weave'

[ʌbé] 'knife'
[ábʲè] 'fat'

p/b
[ʌpé] 'mountain'
[ʌbé] 'monkey'

k͡p/g͡b
[k͡pmá] 'skin'
[g͡bmá] 'pierce'

k/g
[knà] 'fry'
[gnà] 'take off'

g/g͡b
[gnà] 'divide'
[g͡bmá] 'pierce'

j/w
[jáwʲì] 'maize'
[wágʲè] 'sleep'

m/n
[bímà] 'give birth'
[g͡bmínà] 'feather'

v/z
[vàjá] 'all'
[zázã̀] 'walk'

u/o
[zùkʷó] 'hoe'
[zòkʷó] 'pat'

i/u
[sī] 'drink'
[sū] 'swell'

high/mid/low tone
[ʌbé] 'knife' [ʌbe] 'monkey'

3.5.3 Evidence of syllable structure

CV	/sa/ 'bite', /wo/ 'hear', /mi/ 'swallow'
CVN	/kpónkpélè/ 'chin' (only unambiguous example)
CNV	/dná/ 'dwell', /jnágbà/ 'pepper'
CGV	/sjàmá/ 'yam', /wjì/ 'blow', /njàbó/ 'request'
CGNV	/sjnàknú/ 'pot'
ONGV	/ègbnjá/ 'fish', /knji/ 'choose'

3.5.4 Rules

The following rules apply.

Nasal assimilation. The nasal becomes a velar nasal when followed by a back consonant, and a bilabial nasal when preceded by a labial consonant, e.g, /kpónkpélè/ [k͡pʌŋk͡péɹè] 'chin' and /ègbnjá/ [ʌg͡bmʲá] 'fish'.

$$\begin{bmatrix} +\text{syllabic} \\ +\text{nasal} \end{bmatrix} \rightarrow \begin{matrix} [+\text{back}] \\ [+\text{labial}] \end{matrix} \Big/ \begin{matrix} \underline{\quad} \\ [+\text{labial}] \underline{\quad} \end{matrix} \begin{bmatrix} +\text{syllabic} \\ +\text{back} \end{bmatrix}$$

Nasal assimilation on vowels. A vowel may become nasalized when it follows a nasal, e.g., /òmí/ [ʌmĩ́] 'oil' and /àgbmí/ [àg͡bmí] 'intestine'.

$$[+\text{syllabic}] \rightarrow [+\text{nasal}] \Big/ \begin{bmatrix} -\text{syllablic} \\ +\text{nasal} \end{bmatrix} \underline{\quad} \text{(optional)}$$

Coalescence rule for nasals. This rule acts differently in different situations. When the nasal follows a plosive the vowel may or may not be nasalized, and the plosive is usually postnasalized. Sometimes only the vowel will be nasalized. If the nasal is following another type of consonant, only the vowel is nasalized. PAP has only one example of CVN (see §3.5.3), and only one of CṼN ([sìntʌló] 'leaf') so that I have interpreted all [CṼ]'s as /CNV/, e.g., /knúbwà/ [knúbʷa] 'ear' and /jnágbà/ [jág͡bà] 'pepper'.

$$\begin{matrix} C & N & V & \rightarrow & [C^{(n)} & & \tilde{V}] \text{ (optional)} \\ 1 & 2 & 3 & & 1 & \emptyset & 3 \end{matrix}$$

$$\begin{matrix} \text{SD:} & & 1 & 2 & 3 \\ \text{SC:} & & 1 & \emptyset & 3 \\ & & | & & | \\ & & [+\text{nasal}] & & [+\text{nasal}] \end{matrix}$$

Coalescence rule for labialization. Any sequence of consonant plus labial velar glide is realized phonetically as a labialized consonant, /bwádà/ [bʷádà] 'hand'.

```
C    w    V    →    [Cʷ         V]
1    2    3         1     ∅      3

SD:       1    2    3
SC:       1    ∅    3
          |
      [+round]
```

Coalescence rules for palatalization. Any sequence of consonant plus palatal glide is realized phonetically as a palatalized consonant, /èpjá/ [èpʲá] 'moon'.

```
C    j    V    →    [Cʲ    V]
```

The alveolars go one step further, becoming alveopalatal consonants as in /djédà/ [dʲédà] ~ [ʤédà] 'groundnut'.

$$\begin{bmatrix} /tʲ/ \\ /dʲ/ \\ /sʲ/ \\ /zʲ/ \\ /nʲ/ \end{bmatrix} \rightarrow \begin{bmatrix} [tʃ] \\ [ʤ] \\ [ʃ] \\ [ʒ] \\ [ɲ] \end{bmatrix}$$

[lʲ] → [ɹ] (optional)

On [ɓ] and [g͡b]. The labial velar stop becomes implosive word initially when there are no other consonants separating it from the vowel. The only difference between these two phones is in the amount of implosion, and the implosion is greater word initially before a vowel as in /gbà/ [ɓà] 'break', /gbmá/ [g͡bmá] 'pierce'.

/gb/ → [ɓ] / # __ V

On [h]. [h] has a limited occurrence, but it does occur in some common words like the second-person singular pronoun 'you' [ho]. It occurs word initially and medially before vowels, and with the /w/ glide once, in [òhʷá] 'farm'. I believe that it may be allophonic with /f/, as /f/ only occurs word initially with glides, and ARA, the other Gbagyi lect, has [òfʷá] 'farm'. Also, the second person plural pronoun is [ɓe]. If not for 'farm', I would posit the following rule, but at this point more study needs to be done.

/f/ → [h] / __ V

Vowel feature assimilation. The [−low] vowels tend to assimilate to the following consonant when it is [+high] as in /dujá/ [dijá] 'pass by something' and /djègú/ [ʤògú] 'to bark'; but cf. /djékpèjàkó/ [ʤékp̚èjàkó] 'robe'.

$$\begin{bmatrix} +\text{syllabic} \\ +\text{ATR} \\ -\text{low} \\ \alpha\text{back} \end{bmatrix} \rightarrow [-\alpha\text{back}] \ / \ \_\_ \ \begin{bmatrix} -\text{syllabic} \\ +\text{high} \\ -\alpha\text{back} \end{bmatrix}$$

On ATR. The [+ATR] vowels become [−ATR] when they are word medial or word initial and there is no glide of the same value of [back] preceding or following them as in /èsú/ [èsú] 'bee' and /sésí/ [sésí] 'tail'.

$$\begin{bmatrix} +\text{syllabic} \\ \alpha\text{back} \\ \alpha\text{round} \\ +\text{ATR} \end{bmatrix} \rightarrow [-\text{ATR}] \ / \ \left(\begin{bmatrix} -\text{syllabic} \\ -\text{high} \\ -\alpha\text{back} \\ -\alpha\text{round} \end{bmatrix}\right) \_\_ \left\{\begin{bmatrix} -\text{syllabic} \\ -\text{high} \\ -\alpha\text{back} \\ -\alpha\text{round} \end{bmatrix}\right\}$$

3.5.5 Phoneme chart of Northern Gbagyi

Consonants		Labial	Alveolar	Palatal	Velar	Labial velar
Plosive	vl.	p	t		k	kp
	vd.	b	d		g	gb
Fricative	vl.	f	s			
	vd.		z			
Nasal		m	n			
Approximant		l		j	w	

Vowels	Front	Central	Back
High	i		u
Mid	e		o
Low		a	

4
Glides

This chapter discusses one of the more prominent features of the Gwari phonological system, the glide. There are two glides, the palatal glide /j/ and the labial velar glide /w/, both functioning in a similar way in the phonological rules. While they appear at first glance to be predictable, occurring mainly before vowels of the same value of [back] and [round], they contrast before /a/, and occur before vowels of the opposite values of [back] and [round] at least at the phonetic level. At the phonological level they are very important to the vowel system. Phonetically, they serve to soften the sound of the consonants they apply to, making Gwari very pleasant to listen to, with few harsh sounds jarring the ear. Phonologically, they serve as protectors for the vowels or as preservers of the vowel features when the vowels have been forced to assimilate.

4.1 The palatal glide

4.1.1 The phonetic realization of the palatal glide

/j/ is found in Gwari in two positions of the syllable—in the syllable-initial position where it functions like any other consonant except that it does not receive labialization, and in the syllable-medial position discussed below. When /j/ occurs in the syllable-initial position, it can occur with any of the [−round] vowel phonemes. It is nevertheless in contrast with /w/, which can occur with any vowel. This contrast is seen in [ján̄jà] 'dance' and [wà] 'catch' from PAP and in [k͡pájè] 'millet' and [kâwé] 'dry' from GBB.

All Gwari lects are characterized by a good number of consonants with a secondary articulation of palatalization such as [pʲ]. There are also some palatal consonants which may be better analyzed as palatalized consonants, such as [ʤ]→[dʲ]. These kinds of phones can be interpreted in several different ways: as a single phoneme /Cʲ/, or as a sequence of two phonemes either /Ci/ or /Cj/. I have chosen to interpret them as a /Cj/ sequence for the following reasons.

Analyzing them as individual phonemes adds a large number of phonemes to the phonological system, and, as they are realized in two different ways, the basic simplicity of the glide system is obscured. This is especially true since, in different dialects, different palatalized phones are not contrastive. Secondly, if interpreted as /Ci/, there is little unambiguous evidence for a CVV syllable type and the glide carries no tone, having no autonomous realization syllable internally. Also, it would be difficult to explain why /CiV/ is not found for /kp/, /gb/, /ɓ/, or /j/ when they all can be followed by /i/ in the /CV/ syllable.

On the other hand, positing the palatal glide in a /Cj/ structure has a most drastic effect upon the phoneme chart. Among the different lects, palatalization can occur on any consonant phoneme except /kp/, /gb/, /ɓ/, or /j/ itself. It even occurs on the labial velar glide /w/. A simple coalescence rule can account for all of these:

$$C \quad j \quad V \quad \rightarrow \quad [C^j \quad V]$$

[ʲ] is realized differently in different lects and on different phonemes, and some phonemes only rarely have it. Its different phonetic realizations between lects, however, help to substantiate the common phenomenon, especially when this occurs on the same words.

[tʲ] occurs for example, in free variation with [tʃ] in one of the lects, and in the same words where [tʃ] occurs in other lects. [ts], which exists only in one dialect and only occurs before [+round] vowels, occurs only in words which are [tʃu...] or [tʃo...] in other lects.

The palatal glide has its most obvious effect upon the alveolar and alveopalatal series, and it is my belief that they are allophones, such that an alveolar becomes an alveopalatal when followed by a palatal glide. The fact that the alveopalatals never have a palatal glide also argues for their nonphonemic status.

In its role of preserver of the vowel features, the palatal glide's absence predicts [ɪ] and [ɛ] (see §4.1.3). Thus, positing the glide [ʲ] as part of the function of the already existent phoneme /j/ accounts for seventeen different phones ([pʲ, tʲ/tʃ, ts, kʲ, bʲ/βʲ, dʲ/ʤ, gʲ/ɣʲ, fʲ, ʃ, vʲ, ʒ, mʲ, ɲ, lʲ/ɾʲ/ɹʲ, wʲ, ɪ, and ɛ]).

Glides

4.1.2 The distribution of the palatal glide

The following examples demonstrate the distribution of /j/.

pj	[èpʲá]	/èpjá/	'moon'	all
	[èpá]	/èpá/	'urine'	GBB, GIR
tj	[fùntʲé]	/fùntjé/	'leaf'	GIR
	[kàtʲé]	/kàtjé/	'room'	GIR
	[petʃè]	/petjè/	'mat'	ARA
	[tʃígʷò]	/tjígwò/	'head'	GBB
	[fʷátʃùgʷó]	/fwátjùgwó/	'village'	GBB
	[ʌtsǘ]	/òtjú/	'smell'	GIR
	[ʌtú]	/òtú/	'vomit'	GIR
kj	[kʲí]	/kjí/	'sew'	GIR
	[kìnú]	/kìnú/	'sheep'	GIR
	[ʒàkʲí]	/zjàkjí/	'donkey'	PAP
bj	[bʲà]	/bjà/	'blow'	GBB
	[bà]	/bà/	'count'	GBB
	[bʲè]	/bjè/	'sow'	GBB
	[bʲí]	/bjí/	'plant'	GBB
dj	[ʤì]	/djì/	'carve'	ARA
	[díjá]	/dújá/	'pass by'	ARA
	[líʤà]	/lídjìà/	'well'	ARA
	[lídètʃé]	/lídètjé/	'kite'	ARA
gj	[gʲáhù]	/gjáhù/	'fly'	PAP
	[gàwó]	/gàwó/	'give'	PAP
fj	[fʲĩtʌló]	/fjìntóló/	'leaf'	ARA
	[fídàkúlú]	/fíndàkúlú/	'rubbish'	ARA
sj	[áʃì]	/ásjì/	'cough'	ARA
	[ásì]	/ásnì/	'smell'	ARA
	[ʃògʷó]	/sjògwó/	'rain'	GIR
vj	[vʲí]	/vjí/	'follow'	ARA
	[èví]	/èví/	'thief'	ARA

zj	[èʒí]	/èzjí/	'egg'	all
	[ɛzí]	/ezí/	'palm oil'	GIR
	[ʒì]	/zjì/	'come'	GIR
	[zíjà]	/zíjà/	'pour'	GIR
mj	[ʌɡ͡bmʲá]	/ègbmjá/	'fish'	PAP
	[mʲũ̀kũ̀]	/mjùknù/	'hunger'	PAP
nj	[kɲí]	/knjí/	'choose'	PAP
	[ɲàkṹ]	/njàknú/	'room'	PAP
	[náknã̀]	/náknà/	'charcoal'	PAP
	[náwũ̀]	/náwnù/	'extinguish'	PAP
lj	[ɓɛɾè]	/gbóljè/	'many'	GIR
	[ɓàlé]	/gbàlé/	'cat'	GIR
wj	[èwʲé]	/èwjé/	'eye'	all
	[wʲôwʲò]	/wjêwjò/	'cold'	GBB
	[kàwé]	/kàwé/	'dry'	GBB
	[dàwʲé]	/dàwjé/	'want'	GBB
i	[gʲí]	/gjí/	'eat'	all
	[jikala]	/jikala/	'hard'	GIR
e	[fʲègʷósà]	/fjègwósà/	'dawn'	GBB
	[jéknã̀]	/jéknà/	'gather'	GIR, GBB
a	[ʧáʃì]	/tjásjì/	'God'	GIR
	[jàbó]	/jàbó/	'request'	ARA
o	[tsṍngʷó]	/tjóngwó/	'night'	GBB
	[ʤògò]	/djègù/	'bark'	ARA, PAP
u	[bùʒùkʷó]	/bùzjùkwó/	'thigh'	ARA, PAP

4.1.3 The effect of the palatal glide upon vowels

Gwari vowels are very fluid. That is, they are transparent to the features of the following consonant unless they have a protector glide backing them up. The only exception to this is /a/ which rarely changes its features.[4]

---

[4] /a/ is the only [−ATR] phonemic vowel, and perhaps the reason for its stability is that it has already lost its changeable features. It does, rarely, go to [æ] following the palatal glide. This argues for the features of /a/ to be [−ATR], [−high], [−round] and [−back]. Assigning the feature [−back] to /a/ is a controversial issue which I will not pursue here.

Glides 95

To a varying extent from lect to lect, /j/ is the protector and/or preserver of the features of the [−round], [+ATR] vowels, such that they should remain [+ATR] and [−round] when the syllable they are in or the following syllable contains /j/. Note that the rules given below are generalizations for Gwari as a whole, and individual lects may modify them somewhat.

Vowel ATR rule 1. A [+ATR] vowel goes to [−ATR] when it is word initial and followed by a [−high] consonant that does not have a glide. This is exemplified by [èpʲá] /èpjá/ 'moon' in all lects and [èpá] /èpá/ 'urine' GBB, GIR.

$$\begin{bmatrix} +\text{syllabic} \\ +\text{ATR} \end{bmatrix} \rightarrow [-\text{ATR}] \;/\; \# \underline{} \begin{bmatrix} -\text{syllabic} \\ -\text{high} \end{bmatrix} \left(\begin{bmatrix} -\text{syllabic} \\ -\text{high} \end{bmatrix} \right)$$

Vowel ATR rule 2. A [+ATR] vowel goes to [−ATR] when it is word medial and neither the syllable it is in nor the following one contain a glide. When the rule is stated in the above form, it must take effect before the coalescence rules. It is illustrated in [mítàɹà] /mítàɹà/ 'tongue' and [míjasṹ] /míjasnù/ 'stink' GBB.

$$\begin{bmatrix} +\text{syllabic} \\ +\text{ATR} \\ -\text{round} \end{bmatrix} \rightarrow [-\text{ATR}] \;/\; [+\text{Cons}] \underline{} [+\text{Cons}] \;([+\text{Cons}])$$

/j/ is also the aggressor against the [+round] vowels, forcing them to go to [−round] when it is in the following syllable and there is no /w/ in the preceding syllable.

Vowel assimilation rule. A [−low][+back] vowel becomes [−back] when the following consonant is [−back] and [+high], and there is no [+back] glide on the preceding consonant.

$$\begin{bmatrix} +\text{syllabic} \\ +\text{back} \end{bmatrix} \rightarrow [-\text{back}] \;/\; \left(\begin{bmatrix} -\text{syllabic} \\ -\text{high} \end{bmatrix} \right) \underline{} \begin{bmatrix} -\text{syllabic} \\ -\text{back} \\ +\text{high} \end{bmatrix}$$

This rule is illustrated in [díjá] /dújá/ 'pass by' ARA. It is interesting to note that when the situation ... CjVCw ... or ... CwVCj ... exists it becomes a battleground, with the features of the vowel in free variation and indeterminate unless some morphophonemic process allows for the two syllables to split.

However, the vowel features can be deduced from evidence from other dialects: [fʷátʃùgʷó] 'village' GBB can be either /fwátjùgwó/ or /fwátjìgwó/, and [ɲúkʷózà] or [ɲíkʷózà] 'woman' ARA is either /njúkwózà/ or /njíkwózà/. In these cases I have generally assumed that the original vowel had the features of the preceding glide, but that the glide following the vowel proved stronger than the glide preceding it, forcing the assimilation. A [+back] is also apparently stronger than the palatal glide, as vowels in some dialects can assimilate to a following [+back] consonant even if there is no labial velar glide, [ʤògù] /djègù/ 'to bark' ARA.[5] In any case, the palatal glide retains the features of [−back], [−round] and [+ATR]/[+high] if and when the vowel loses them.

4.2 The labial velar glide

4.2.1 The phonetic realization of the labial velar glide

Although labialization does not occur on quite as many consonants as palatalization does, its use is just as widespread. Regardless of the position of the labial velar glide, it can occur with any of the vowel phonemes. When it is in the syllable-initial position, it behaves like any other consonant, even receiving palatalization. In the syllable-medial position it occurs following all the consonant phonemes except the alveolars, [ɓ], [k͡p], and [w] itself. It does occur with one alveolar, /s/. [ʷ] has the same function as [ʲ], i.e., phonetically it softens the consonant it occurs on, and phonemically it is the protector and preserver of the [+round] vowels.

There is no problem with the phonemic status of the /w/ in the syllable initial position because its distribution is complete and it is in contrast with all other possible allophones (see §4.2.2). In the syllable medial position, however, the same three interpretations that are given for /j/ are possible— the labialized consonants can be phonemes, they can be sequences of /Cu/, or they can be consonant clusters of /Cw/. Again, I have chosen the third interpretation.

The same arguments apply for /Cw/ as did for /Cj/, and perhaps even more strongly. Interpreting [Cʷ] as /Cʷ/ would add a heavy burden to the phoneme chart, and since /w/ must be a phoneme, there would be no compensation. The syllable structure would still be complex since the /Cʷ/ would have to be individually specified in reference to the nasals, i.e.,

---

[5]See §4.2.3 for a further note on this word.

Glides 97

[C^wN] and [CʲN] do not occur. In reference to the /Cu/ sequence, again, Gwari has no unambiguous CVV's, the /u/ never carries tone, and there is no reason why CuV shouldn't occur with every phoneme that Cu occurs with.

/Cw/, on the other hand, seems to express the phenomenon of labialization most simply, and when the processes of palatalization and nasalization are compared with it, a real harmony of the three processes is apparent. /Cw/ is perhaps the simplest of the three in that the phonetic representation of labial velar glide is consistent on every consonant in every lect, and it does not force the reinterpretation of any series (like /j/ does for the alveopalatals). This rule is similar to the palatal glide coalescence rule.

$$\begin{array}{ccccccc} C & w & V & \rightarrow & [C^w & & V] \\ 1 & 2 & 3 & & 1 & \emptyset & 3 \end{array}$$

SD: 1 2 3
SC: 1 ∅ 3
     |
  [+round]

Thus, positing the labial velar glide can account for thirteen phones [p^w, k^w, b^w/β^w, g^w/ɣ^w, ɠb^w, f^w/ɸ^w, s^w, h^w, v^w, m^w, n^w/ŋ^w, ʊ, and ʌ]. (See §4.2.3 for an explanation of [ʊ] and [ʌ].)

4.2.2 The distribution of the labial velar glide

The following is a description of the distribution of /w/.

pw	[p^wákū]	/pwáknu/	'bag'	PAP
	[p^wo]	/pwo/	'mould'	GBB
	[pò]	/pò/	'wash'	GBB
	[kàp^wí]	/kàpwí/	'crab'	GIR, GBB, PAP
	[ápì]	/apì/	'compound'	PAP
kw	[k^wíjà]	/kwójà/	'kneel'	GIR
	[kìnú]	/kìnú/	'sheep'	GIR
	[zòk^wob^wá]	/zòk^wobwá/	'press'	ARA
bw	[b^wíjà]	/bwójà/	'spit'	GBB
	[bì]	/bì/	'bury'	GBB
	[ʌ̀b^wé]	/ɛ̀bwé/	'calabash'	PAP
	[ʌ̀bé]	/òbé/	'knife'	PAP

ɓw	[ɓʷá]	/ɓwá/	'get'	ARA
	[ɓá]	/ɓá/	'break'	ARA
	[ɓʷí]	/ɓwí/	'lose'	ARA
gw	[gʷo]	/gwo/	'take'	GIR
	[go]	/go/	'grind'	GIR
	[dògʷú]	/dògwú/	'bark'	GIR
	[ógù]	/ógù/	'fight'	GIR
gbw	[gbʷálàgbʷálà]	/gbwálàgbwálà/	'warm'	PAP
	[gbʷo]	/gbwo/	'rotten'	GBB
fw	[ʌfʷi]	/èfwí/	'to die'	PAP
	[òfʷá]	/òfwá/	'farm'	ARA, GIR, GBB
sw	[sʷáʃè]	/swásjè/	'God'	GBB
hw	[òhʷá]	/òfwá/	'farm'	PAP
vw	[ʌvʷí]	/èvwí/	'thief'	PAP
	[vʷì̃]	/vwìn/	'follow'	PAP
mw	[àmʷí]	/àmwí/	'sand'	ARA
	[àmí]	/àmi/	'defecate'	ARA
	[mʷítú]	/mwítú/	'learn'	ARA
	[mítà]	/mítà/	'grinding stone'	ARA
nw	[ŋʷà̃]	/nwà/	'catch'	GIR
	[nàgʷí]	/nàgwin/	'hot'	GIR
	[tnṹŋʷè̃]	/tnúnwè/	'six'	GIR
i	[kã̀wí]	/knàwí/	'thorn'	PAP
e	[wêwê]	/wêwê/	'new'	PAP
a	[wá]	/wá/	'request'	GIR
o	[wó]	/wó/	'hear'	all
u	[wú]	/wú/	'show'	all

4.2.3 The effect of the labial velar glide upon vowels

/w/ has exactly the same effect upon the [+round] ([−low]) vowels that /j/ has upon the [−round] [−low] vowels. It is the protector and preserver of their features. It also acts against the [−round] [−low] vowels, forcing

Glides

them to assimilate when the /j/ is not present (and sometimes even when it is present).

Vowel ATR rule 1. A [+ATR] vowel goes to [−ATR] when it is word initial and followed by a [−high] consonant that does not have a glide. This is exemplified by [ʌbé] /òbé/ 'knife' and [òbʷà] /òbʷà/ 'nose' from Pappanna.

$$\begin{bmatrix} +\text{syllabic} \\ +\text{ATR} \end{bmatrix} \rightarrow [-\text{ATR}] \,/\, \# \underline{} \begin{bmatrix} -\text{syllabic} \\ -\text{high} \end{bmatrix} \left(\begin{bmatrix} -\text{syllabic} \\ -\text{high} \end{bmatrix} \right)$$

Vowel ATR rule 2. A [+ATR] vowel goes to [−ATR] when it is word medial and neither the syllable it is in nor the following one contain a glide. When the rule is stated in the above form, it must apply before the coalescence rules. [kʷíjà] /kwójà/ 'kneel' and [kìnú] /kìnú/ 'sheep' from GIR.

$$\begin{bmatrix} +\text{syllabic} \\ +\text{ATR} \\ +\text{round} \end{bmatrix} \rightarrow [-\text{ATR}] \,/\, [+\text{Cons}] \underline{} [+\text{Cons}] \,([+\text{Cons}])$$

Vowel assimilation rule. A [−low] [−back] vowel becomes [+back] when the following consonant is [+back] and [+high], and there is no [−back] glide on the preceding consonant. This can be seen in [dògʷù] /dègwù/ 'to bark' GIR. It is difficult to discover the original vowels in this rule, except that two syllable verbs often switch the order of their syllables, such that /gwúdè/ also means 'to bark'. [ɸègʷósà] /fjègwósà/ 'dawn' GBB is an example where the palatal glide has prevented the vowel from assimilating, and [ɲű́gʷò] ~ [ɲíg̃ʷò] 'wife' GBB where the two glides are of apparently equal strength.

$$\begin{bmatrix} +\text{syllabic} \\ -\text{back} \end{bmatrix} \rightarrow [+\text{back}] \,/\, \left(\begin{bmatrix} -\text{syllabic} \\ -\text{high} \end{bmatrix} \right) \underline{} \begin{bmatrix} -\text{syllabic} \\ +\text{back} \\ +\text{high} \end{bmatrix}$$

5
Nasality

Nasalization is another process which is rather complicated in Gwari, and while there are still a lot of questions about it, it appears to have the same status as the glides and to require recognition in the syllable structure. While it functions differently than the glides by its very nature, it affects them and the interaction between the two can be complicated. I first discuss the distribution of nasality in the four lects (examples are found in chapter two) and then proffer my own observations and tentative solution.

5.1 The distribution and phonetic manifestations of nasality

Nasality is realized phonetically in three ways in all the dialects. It is realized as a nasal consonant, a postnasalized consonant, and a nasalized vowel.

5.1.1 The nasal consonants

There are two nasal consonants in Gwari, /m/ and /n/.

Syllable initial position. In the syllable initial position, the nasal consonants not only contrast, but can be palatalized ([mʲ] and [ɲ]), and labialized ([mʷ] and [ŋʷ]). These phones behave in the same way as any other syllable initial consonant, except that they do not receive nasalization, which would, of course, be redundant. They are contrastive with each other, and with their oral counterparts, as illustrated in the following examples from GBB.

[mà]	'lick'	[nágbájì]		'hunter'
[bà]	'count'	[dàgbá]		'elephant'
[mì]	'swallow'	[dàgbmá]		'older brother'
[bì]	'bury'	[ɲì]	/nji/	'dig'
		[ʤì]	/dji/	'give'

/m/ and /n/ both occur in the syllable initial position in every lect, word initially, and word medially. The glides, /w/ and /j/, occur following the syllable initial /m/ and /n/ word initially and word medially. I did not find evidence, however, for /nw/ in GBB at all, or in PAP word initially. The occurrence of the glides with /m/ is limited to precede particular vowels. /j/ occurs only before /a/ and /u/, while /w/ occurs only before /a/ and /i/. With /n/, the palatal glide /j/ is predictable before [−back] vowels, but also occurs with [+back] vowels, while /w/ occurs rarely, but is found with /e/, /a/, and /u/ in various lects.

The high and low vowels occur freely following both /m/ and /n/, but the mid vowels occur much more rarely, limited even in the NGV structure. I found no example of a mid vowel following a nasal in GBB, while the other lects only have one or two examples each.

Nasalized vowels can follow syllable initial /m/ and /n/ and can also follow /mG/ and /nG/. Oral vowels also occur in the same positions, and are more frequent.

Syllable final position. Nasal consonants also occur, rarely, syllable finally, although they are never found on the surface word finally. These nasals, however, assimilate to the following consonant in place of articulation, and there is no contrast between /m/ and /n/ preconsonantally, i.e., [kamba] 'wall' and [kpáŋkpéɹe] 'chin' PAP.

Although syllable-final nasals occur at the phonetic level only word medially, they are analyzed as syllable final because NCV is not a syllable structure attested to in Gwari. Although they are not common, they occur in every lect. They only occur before plosives (including the implosive), and in ARA and PAP, they only follow nasalized vowels. They occur following both oral and nasal vowels in GIR and GBB, and they can follow mid vowels. Syllable final nasals do not receive palatalization, but there is some question with labialization on /n/, i.e., [ŋʷ] word medially could be either a labialized nasal or a nasalized labial velar (or both). In any case, ... VNGCV ... never occurs.

Nasality

5.1.2 The postnasalized consonants

Postnasalized consonants have been represented in this thesis by the syllable structure CN. CN is manifested in a number of ways phonetically. Word initially, it can be [CⁿV] or [CʰV] or even [CṼ]. Word medially, it is more often [CNV] than anything else.

Every lect has examples of [tn], [kn], [k͡pm], [dɲ], [gn], and [g͡bm] (or [ɓm]) which occur syllable initially, and word initially or medially. They are never followed by mid vowels, and can rarely be followed by a glide. I only found one example of a labial velar glide following a postnasalized consonant: [ʃíg͡bmʷàgùlù] 'tree bark' GBB. Any vowel can precede these consonants word medially, and there is an example of a nasal preceding [Gbm] in GIR, [wʲedʒiŋg͡bmà] 'darkness'. The palatal glide is more frequent, and occurs in every lect, as in [kɲàɹí] /knjàljí/ 'red' GIR.

5.1.3 The nasal(ized) vowels

Nasal(ized) vowels occur most often in the company of a nasal consonant or a postnasalized consonant. Free fluctuation occurs between [CNV] and [CṼ] with /tn/, /kn/, and /gn/, i.e., /knúbwà/ 'ear' is found as [knúbʷà] ~ [kṹbʷà]. They also occur, however, when there is no other nasal present. They occur without the presence of other nasals most commonly word finally, where there is a contrast between them and the oral vowels, as in [si] 'buy' and [sĩ̀] 'drink', and [ʃi] 'plant' and [ʃĩ̀] 'descend' from GIR. Word medially, Ṽ and ṼN are often in free fluctuation as in [gʷúʒèdá] ~ [gʷúʒẽ̀ndá] 'witch' ARA. I found no contrast between CNV, CNṼ, and CṼ. I have no examples of word-initial nasalized vowels, although Hyman and Magaji (1970) give an example of a grammatical particle /in/ which is nasalized. They do not indicate if it can stand alone.

5.2 Phonological interpretations of nasality

5.2.1 Nasality and consonants

The existence of two phonemic nasal consonants /m/ and /n/ is easily argued. In the syllable initial position they are contrastive, not only with each other, but with /b/ and /d/; they behave in the same way as any other syllable initial consonant, receiving palatalization and labialization, except that they don't receive nasalization. Also, although vowels can be nasalized following a syllable initial nasal, they remain oral more often than not, as was evidenced in the preceding examples.

The presence of phonemic nasal consonants in the syllable final position is more ambiguous, however, and a number of different interpretations are possible. The fact that they never occur phonetically word finally is one of the larger problems, while the facts that they usually follow nasalized vowels and assimilate to the following consonant (and thus do not contrast with each other) also cause difficulties.

Syllable final nasal consonants (... VNC... and ... ṼNC...) could be interpreted to be the product of the nasalized vowel, such that they would be ... ṼC... phonemically, or they could be interpreted as phonemic nasal consonants. The third possible interpretation would be that they are really syllable initial consonants, but this interpretation has little plausibility given the fact that it is not attested to word initially and that the nature of the consonant clusters is already complex enough.

The argument that they are the result of nasalized vowels is more plausible, except for the fact that they can also follow oral vowels, which would require a loss of nasalization rule to be introduced with no other motivation. Also, the syllable-final nasals can follow mid vowels as in [pùsémɓà] 'cock' GIR, which are not normally nasalized. A third reason is that, while the nasals do assimilate to the following consonant, particularly following oral vowels, they are not merely transitions between the vowel and the consonant, but have their own timing allotment.

The best interpretation is, I believe, that they are syllable final nasal consonants. Although this interpretation requires a CVN syllable structure, the fact that they follow oral vowels and mid vowels seems to indicate this solution, as a loss of nasalization rule does not seem warranted. The absence of any other syllable-final consonant makes the argument a little more ambiguous, but other Nupoid languages also have the syllable-final position restricted to vowels and nasals. Also, it would not be difficult to introduce a rule as follows, requiring word-final nasals to be deleted, passing their nasality onto the preceding vowel.

Nasality coalescence rule 1

	V	N	#	→	[Ṽ		#]
	1	2	3		1	∅	3
SD:		1	2		3		
SC:		1	∅		3		

[+nasal]

This rule helps as well with problems in analyzing the postnasalized consonants.

They can be interpreted as phones /Cⁿ/, CN sequences, or CṼ sequences. I am undecided as to which is the best interpretation but have chosen to interpret them as CN sequences in the rest of this volume. Interpreting them as /Cⁿ/ or CṼ would help to simplify the syllable structure somewhat, but would add a number of phones to the phoneme chart. While it is less drastic than that of the glides, it is perhaps unnecessary. Arguing for /Cⁿ/ would also anchor the nasality to the consonant and thus distinguish it from the nasality found on the vowels which would perhaps be unfortunate.

Interpreting them as consonants followed by nasalized vowels is a better solution, and one which would have support from the language family. In Nupe, apparent cognates with Gwari generally have nasalized vowels where Gwari has postnasalized consonants.[6] Also, some of the Gwari lects have the same limitation on nasalized vowels that is found in Nupe such that mid vowels are never nasal, and [Cⁿ] never occurs before these vowels, while /m/ and /n/ do. This solution could even be combined with the nasal vowel solution for syllable final consonants above, to result in nasal consonants only occurring word initially, and nasal vowels occurring anywhere but word initially.

One problem with this solution, however, is that the vowels in the CNV sequence are not necessarily nasal, and one would again have to posit a loss of nasality rule for these vowels when there doesn't appear to be much motivation for it, and if one were to combine the two solutions, there would be no way of predicting which direction nasality would spread. Also, the occurrence of the glides following postnasalized consonants effectively gives the nasal autonomy from the vowel.

Interpreting them as CN is helpful in that it allows for more flexibility in the syllable structure. Having the nasals as autonomous segments means that they are not always connected with either a consonant or a vowel. These nasals also receive the palatal glide, as in /ègbmjà/ 'fish' and /èknjí/ 'ground' PAP, (and labial velar glide, see above), thus separating them from the vowel.

If this third interpretation is taken, other consonants besides the stops may be included in the CN syllable structure. This could actually be used as the primary way of representing nasality except that there are a few problems. Hyman and Shekwo both favor, for example, representing [sĩ] as |sni| rather than |sin|. The problem comes with [ʃĩ] 'descend' GIR ([sĩ] 'drink' also occurs in GIR). While it could be represented as /ʃni/ in an analysis which has a phonemic /ʃ/, it would have to be represented as /sjni/

---

[6]Hyman and Magaji (1970:7).

in my analysis as the nasality does not precede the glide. Examples of this were found in all of the dialects I studied.

This problem could perhaps be an argument for keeping the alveopalatals phonemic, as it forces the inclusion of another syllable structure CGNV (CNGV is already listed), or CGVN unless there are phonemic nasal vowels. CGVN is not too difficult, however, especially if one accepts the phonemic existence of syllable final nasals. There would only need to be a structural constraint that CGN does not occur.

Orthographically, however, both Shekwo and Hyman prefer that the nasal precede the vowel, although they both have had trouble doing that consistently. Shekwo, in personal conversation, argues for the existence of both /jn/ and /nj/, and cites the examples of /àjní/ 'world', /ánjì/ 'soup', /ònjí/ 'hernia', and /òjní/ 'termite'. I believe the phonetic representations would be [àjĩ], [áɲì], [òɲí], and [òjĩ], respectively.

Hyman prefers CNV and CNGV to CVN and CGVN because it allows for a more practical representation of reduplication, i.e., /knú/ 'to sell' is reduplicated as /knuknui/ which is much closer to the phonetic manifestation than /kunkuni/.[7] I have no problem with this structure, except that it adds to the already numerous types of syllable structures possible. I believe that CVN must still be kept as a syllable type, at least for those syllable final nasals which follow oral vowels. A more detailed study of this is warranted, especially morphophonemically.

5.2.2 Nasality and vowels

There are two options for the interpretation of nasality in relation to the vowels. Either there are phonemic nasal vowels, or phonemically oral vowels which receive nasalization from the nasal consonants. I am undecided on this issue also, but I have taken the position that there are no phonemic nasal vowels in Gwari.

As stated earlier, one could argue for both the syllable-final nasals and the nasality on postnasalized consonants to be the products of processes acting on the nasal vowels, except that the occurrence of oral vowels with both types of phones makes this analysis difficult, as does the fact that the spread of nasality, and even its direction is unpredictable. On the other hand, given the existence of syllable-final nasals and postnasalized consonants, nasalized vowels occur alone very rarely. And, if we accept the nasality coalescence rule for word-final nasals, perhaps a similar one for syllable-final but word-medial consonants is also in order as follows.

---

[7]Hyman and Magaji (1970:13).

Nasality

Nasality coalescence rule 2

```
V   N   C   →   [Ṽ       C]  (optional)
1   2   3       1    ∅   3
SD:     1   2   3
SC:     1   ∅   3
        |
      [+nasal]
```

This rule would have to be optional, given the existence of word-medial, syllable-final nasals, and it would only be partially in effect in some instances, i.e., the ones where there is a nasalized vowel preceding the nasal, but it would help to explain why all three situations exist, i.e., ...VNC..., ...ṼNC... and ...ṼC...

Another rule would also have to be introduced to deal with postnasalized consonants. This rule would be applied in varying degrees, dependent upon the consonant involved, and there would be some optionality of use which appears to characterize nasality in Gwari generally.

Nasality coalescence rule 3

```
C   N   V   →   [C⁽ⁿ⁾       Ṽ]  (optional)
1   2   3       1       ∅   3
SD:     1   2   3
SC:     1   ∅   3
        |           |
    [+nasal]    [+nasal]
```

This appears to me to be the best solution. The nasality on the vowels is just as elusive and varying as their ATR, and their value of [back]. Also, it would be necessary to posit different nasal vowel phonemes in different lects if vowels were phonemically nasal, as GIR has both mid vowels nasalized, GBB has [õ], ARA has [ẽ], and PAP has only high and low vowels nasalized. Otherwise, all that is needed is a lect-specific constraint for which vowels can receive nasalization.

5.3 Nasality and the syllable structure

In conclusion, I have interpreted nasality in Gwari to be a feature of the nasal consonants which can spread to the vowels. The two nasal consonants /m/ and /n/ contrast with each other only syllable initially, but they also occur following other consonants, and syllable finally. The vowel can assimilate in nasality with any nasal consonant, and carries the nasality of the nasal consonant when the consonant is deleted.

This interpretation indicates the syllable structures below (examples are taken from GBB).

N	/n̄wá/	'need'
NV	/máɹì/	'good'
NGV	/mwàɹí/	'horn'
ONV	/k͡pmà/ 'take off' (/sní/ 'drink')	
ONGV	/knjàɹí/	'red'
OVN	/kàmba/ 'maize' (/sín/ 'drink')	
OGVN (or OGNV)	/gjínɹín/ /gjníɹní/ 'mortar'	
	/sjìn/ /sjnì/ 'descend'	

6
Unity of Gwari—Gbagyi and Gbari

Although there is a marked unity between the Gwari lects phonologically, this unity is not apparent elsewhere. In fact, having begun this study with lexical counts and sociolinguistic questionnaires, I was expecting a far greater degree of difference phonologically, and was pleasantly surprised not to find it.

6.1 Sociological unity

While the Gwari are very similar culturally throughout Gwariland, language attitudes have served to limit their unity as a people. Although I was not doing a cultural study, which would perhaps have turned up more differences, the only things I noted were that the style of the dwelling changed somewhat from north to south and from Gbagyi to Gwari, and that the Gbari are the more isolated and less advantaged of the two groups.

The Gbagyi are the most unified of the Gwari. They value their unity as a people and seek to promote it. While they recognize differences in speech in the Gbagyi dialects from north to south, and can even describe them with examples, they are quick to say "We are all one people." They include the Gbari in this claim, although they admit that they cannot understand the Gbari speech. They generally make no attempt to learn Gbari, expecting the Gbari to learn Gbagyi instead. In general, they believe that the Gbari are Gbagyi who have allowed their language to become mixed with Nupe and Hausa.

The Gbari, however, are not so quick to claim unity with the Gbagyi. Part of the reason is that the Gbari are usually much more isolated than the Gbagyi, and do not even seek unity among themselves. The Gbari have little knowledge about other Gwari villages outside of their state, or even their local government area, not even knowing of their existence, to say anything about their relative intelligibility. There are many more monolingual Gbari's, though the Gbagyi have their share as well, particularly southwest of Kaduna.

While some Gbari do learn Gbagyi, particularly in the Federal Capital Territory where the communities are closer together, most do not, and the Northern Gbari in particular do not appreciate being spoken to in Gbagyi. They prefer Hausa over Gbagyi if Gbari cannot be used.

The Northern Gbari, where the lect is most fragmented, are conscious of the differences which can be noted within a half-hour drive, and use them to identify one another, choosing to maximize rather than minimize them. When they have an opinion about the Gbagyi, some will say that they are the same, but others believe the Gbagyi to be a different people, with a different "mother and father."

This is born out by the origin stories. The Gbagyi say that at least their kings are from the Beriberi, while the Gbari trace their origin back to Sokoto.

6.2 Phonological unity—A recommendation for standardization

Phonologically the Gwari lects differ little from each other. The main phonetic differences come from [ɹ] and [l], [g͡b] and [ɓ], and [ts] and [θ], but these are not so drastic phonologically. The basic rules apply to all of the lects, and there are a few lect-specific rules which must be added, but except for /ɓ/ and /ɹ/, the same chart of phonemes can be used for each lect.

This is encouraging and leads to the conclusion that a single standard Gwari orthography is possible if one adds some lect-specific notes for pronunciation. Of course, I haven't dealt with tone, which, by all reports, varies from lect to lect, but it is possible that it can be dealt with in the same ways as the lexicon.

6.3 On lexical counts and intelligibility

It is at the lexical level that intelligibility begins to break down. The Summer Institute of Linguistics, which specializes in producing literature for minority languages, uses apparent cognate counts from word lists as an initial indication of intelligibility between lects and therefore their status as

Unity of Gwari—Gbagyi and Gbari

dialects or languages. They say that a lexical similarity of seventy percent or above indicates that the lects involved are dialects, while a lower percentage of similarity indicates that they are probably languages, but that further testing should be done. As shown in the lexical count chart below, the lexical similarity between Gbagyi and Gwari is between sixty-six percent and seventy-eight percent, right in the area of ambiguity. This is in agreement also with the conflicting opinions on intelligibility which I came across.

Gwari lexical counts based on 170 words

			GWA-SR									
95			GIR-SR									
95	98		KUT-SR									
95	96	96	LED-SR									
81	84	84	86	GBB-NR								
76	79	79	81	87	BAR-NR							
78	81	81	84	86	89	LAS-NR						
75	78	78	81	84	86	86	TUK-NR					
70	72	72	74	74	74	78	78	JAT-NG				
69	70	71	73	72	72	75	74	90	KAR-SG			
67	69	69	72	70	72	75	73	91	90	KAU-NG		
67	68	68	71	70	72	73	72	89	97	89	ORO-SG	
67	68	68	71	71	71	74	72	89	96	90	98	KUR-SG
67	68	68	72	70	71	74	72	91	95	92	96	98 USH-SG
68	68	68	72	72	71	73	72	89	94	89	95	97 96 ARA-SG
66	67	67	71	69	69	72	70	89	92	91	93	92 94 94 RGB-NG
67	68	68	71	71	69	72	73	89	91	91	93	94 93 94 93 PAP-NG

Note: The first three letters above each column are the code letters for the village in which the word list was taken and match the code letters found on the map on the following page. The two letters following the hyphen indicate the lect of the village, i.e., SR is Southern Gbari, NR is Northern Gbari, SG is Southern Gbagyi, and NG is Northern Gbagyi.

Because of this ambiguity I also did recorded-text testing as described in Casad 1974. Recorded-text testing is a method of testing intelligibility where nontraditional three to five minute stories are recorded in various villages, and are played back in other villages. Ten individuals are asked to listen to the tapes and answer questions regarding the stories they hear. The number of correct answers indicates how well the people in that village understand the speech of the village where the story was taped. There are numerous safeguards to insure reliability and validity, and the test has been used successfully for a number of years.

Lexical similarity mapped out

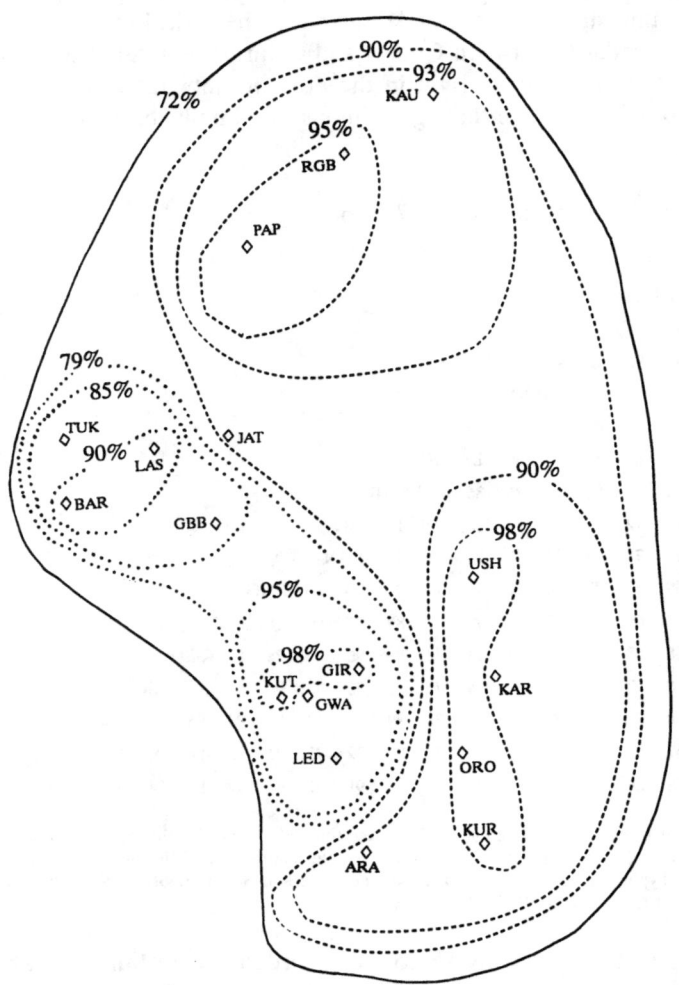

Key
Gwari ———
Gbari ··········
Gbagyi ----------

Percentages are apparent cognate percentages (see lexical count chart on previous page) adjusted for lexical significance.

Unity of Gwari—Gbagyi and Gbari

Because of a time limitation, the indication that the Gbari understood the Gbagyi better than the Gbagyi understood them, and the fact that lexical similarity between the Gbagyi dialects was quite high, I only tested the Gbari's understanding of Gbagyi and the other Gbari lect. My methodology also differed from the standard recorded-text testing methodology in that the questions were asked orally rather than dubbed directly onto the tape. Although this perhaps introduced a certain element of variability into the test, it was found necessary because the people being tested did not recognize or respond to the dubbed questions.

For this test, a score of seventy-five percent or above generally indicates that the lects in question are dialects, while less than seventy-five percent indicates that they are languages. The tapes were played in Chikona, a Northern Gbari village, and Leda, a Southern Gbari village, while the tapes were from ARA, PAP, GBB, and KAT (Kato, a Northern Gbari village). The scores for each village are given below.

Chikona (Northern Gbari)				Leda (Southern Gbari)	
GBB	KAT	ARA	PAP	GBB	ARA
97%	96%	51%	42%	84%	43%

As can be seen, the level of intelligibility is very low between the Gbari and Gbagyi, while it is much higher within the Gbari dialects. This testing is obviously still incomplete, but results so far give a good indication of the general situation.

6.4 Conclusion

It appears to me, that, because of the phonological unity of Gwari, a standard orthography is a definite possibility, but that the lexical differences and the resultingly low level of intelligibility will make it difficult to introduce standardization beyond the phonological level. Also, no investigation that I know of has been done on the grammatical differences between Gbagyi and Gbari and that may introduce further difficulties. It is hoped that this volume will help others as they study the complexities of Gwari.

References

Blench, Roger M. 1987. Nupoid. In John Bendor-Samuel (ed.), The Niger-Congo languages, 305–322. Lanham, Maryland: University Press of America.
Casad, Eugene H. 1974. Dialect intelligibility testing. Publications in linguistics and related fields 38. Norman, Oklahoma: Summer Institute of Linguistics.
Edgar, F. 1909. A grammar of the Gbari language, with Gbari-English and English-Gbari dictionaries. Belfast: W. and G. Laird.
Hansford, Keir, John Bendor-Samuel, and Ron Stanford. 1976. An index of Nigerian languages. Language Data Africa Series 13. Horsleys Green, England: Summer Institute of Linguistics.
Hyman, Larry M. 1975. Phonology: Theory and analysis. New York: Holt, Rinehart and Winston.
——— and Daniel J. Magaji. 1970. Essentials of Gwari grammar. Occasional publication 27. Ibadan, Nigeria: University of Ibadan.
Living Bibles International. 1987. ã6o wowii n ĩesu 6o da ('Great Things Jesus Did'). Enugu, Nigeria.
———. 1987. ã6o wowoii n ĩesu 6o zhin ('Great things Jesus said'). Enugu, Nigeria.
Low, W. P. 1908. Gbari grammar, notes and vocabulary. Zungeru: Government Printer.
Magaji, Daniel, Nuhu Baraje, Musa Yarima, and Nana Bmyanyiko. 1988. Anyajekwu Kmisnui. (A numeracy primer prepared by the Ministry of Education). Ibadan, Nigeria: University Press.
Na'Ibi, Mallam Shuaibu and Alhaji Hassan. 1969. The Gwari, Gade and Koro tribes. Ibadan, Nigeria: University Press.

Sanda, Danladi D. 1986. Gbagyi orthography. In Robert G. Armstrong (ed.), Orthographies of Nigerian languages manual IV, 101–113. Lagos, Nigeria: Federal Ministry of Education.

Shekwo, J. A. 1979. Fundamentals of the Gbagyi language. Zaria, Nigeria: Ahmadu Bello University.

———. 1984. Gbagyi folktales and myths. Vol. 1. Abuja, Nigeria: Garkida Press.

———. 1986a. A series of articles on the Gwari. March 20 to April 10, 1986. The African Guardian, Nigeria.

———. 1986b. Gbagyi: Counting and numbering. Zaria, Nigeria: EMG and Co. Ltd.

———. 1987. Gbagyi spelling book: The common clusters. Zaria, Nigeria: Ahmadu Bello University.

S.I.M. 1956. Anyi Littafi. (Gbagyi hymn book). Jos: The Niger Press, Nigeria.

———. 1956. Al-Haji Kristi Nya. (Pilgrim's Progress). Jos, Nigeria: The Niger Press.

Temple, C. L. 1919, 1965. Notes on the tribes and emirates of Northern Nigeria.

Westermann, Diedrich and M. A. Bryan. 1952, 1970. Languages of West Africa. Handbook of African languages Part II. London: Dawsons of Pall Mall for the International African Institute.

Williamson, Kay. 1989. Niger-Congo Overview. In John Bendor-Samuel (ed.), The Niger-Congo languages, 3–45. Lanham, Maryland: University Press of America.

———. 1989. Benue-Congo overview. In John Bendor-Samuel (ed.), The Niger-Congo languages, 247–274. Lanham, Maryland: University Press of America.

www.ingramcontent.com/pod-product-compliance
Lightning Source LLC
Chambersburg PA
CBHW051103230426
43667CB00013B/2421